Charleville
Sedan

uvers-sur-Seine

PARIS

Seine R.
Troyes

Colmar

Vix
Châtillon-
sur-Seine

Rhine R.

Vézelay

Dijon

Saône R.

Autun

Loire R.

LYONS

Côte d'Arey
Vienne

Le Puy

CÉVENNES MTS.

Rhône R.

Tarn R.

Orange

Tarascon
Avignon
Glanon

Villefranche

Èze

Nîmes
St. Remy-en-Provence
LesBaux

Montpellier
THE
CAMARGUE

Monte Carlo

Mont St. Victoire

arcassonne

Aix
Entremont

Nice

Aigues Mortes

St. Maximin

Antibes

bi

Les Saintes Maries

MARSEILLES

gur

MEDITERRANEAN
SEA

CORSICA

THE SPLENDOR OF FRANCE

BOOKS BY ROBERT PAYNE

THE SPLENDOR OF FRANCE

THE SPLENDOR OF ISRAEL

THE SPLENDOR OF GREECE

THE SPLENDOR OF PERSIA

THE SHEPHERD

THE WHITE RAJAHS OF SARAWAK

THE GOLD OF TROY

THE HOLY FIRE

THE HOLY SWORD

THE WHITE PONY

FOREVER CHINA

THE SPLENDOR

BY ROBERT PAYNE

HARPER & ROW, PUBLISHERS

NEW YORK, EVANSTON, AND LONDON

OF FRANCE

FIRST EDITION   M–N   LIBRARY OF CONGRESS CATALOG CARD NUMBER: 62–20112

CONTENTS

viii CONTENTS

ILLUSTRATIONS

These illustrations, printed as a separate section, will be found following page 52

These illustrations will be found following page 116

Le Puy
French Embassy Press and Information Division
Carcassonne
French Government Tourist Office
Aigues-Mortes
French Government Tourist Office
Chartres Cathedral
French Cultural Services, New York
Abbey Church of Saint Denis
French Cultural Services, New York
The Treasures of Saint Denis
Caisse Nationale des Monuments Historiques and
National Gallery of Art, Washington, D.C.
Montségur
Photo Reportage Yan, Toulouse

These illustrations will be found following page 148

Virgin of Toulouse, Musée des Augustins
Photo Reportage Yan, Toulouse
Saint Louis
Musée de Cluny
Saint Joan of Arc from fifteenth-century manuscript
Bronze Christ at Saint Sernin, Toulouse
Photo Reportage Yan, Toulouse
Christ, from Isenheim Altar
Braun and Cie, Mulhouse
The Blue Virgin of Chartres
La Dame à la Licorne
Musée de Cluny
Constantin Brancusi: Bird in Space
Photo: Museum of Modern Art, New York

THE SPLENDOR OF FRANCE

THE SPLENDOR

I threw open the windows at the *Chèvre d'Or* in Eze, a small hilltop town in the south of France, and there were the blue sea stretching below and the pinewoods going down to the sea's edge, and the sun coming up. It was one of those mornings when everything seems fresh and pure, in the blue misty quivering silence of dawn, silent and untroubled as a forest pool, and there was a sweetness in the air as of stolen fruit. The cool winds of the uplands rustled among the pines, and some white birds were floating serenely in the upper air. Far, far below lay Cap Ferrat like the head of a green swimmer making his way out to sea. It was still so early in the morning that there was no sign of any habitation, no houses, no fishing boats, no one wandering along the pinewood paths: only the silence and the immense blue sea in the arms of the shadowy cliffs.

So it had been before, every time I visited Eze—the sense of splendor welling out of the sea in the gentleness of the morning light. On the rockbound pinnacle of Eze you are hardly more than a stone's throw from Monte Carlo and the naval port of Villefranche, but both are mercifully hidden from sight. The sea-scented air rises into the hills, and it is very quiet there in the narrow streets where the houses have five-feet-thick walls, and perhaps it was even quieter in the Middle Ages when the town was a *lazaretto*, inhabited only by lepers. In those days baskets of food were pushed through a gate in the outer

1

wall, and the lepers were left to fend for themselves. Enviable people, to spend their lives on this high fortress overlooking the sea!

Soon the freshness of the morning light was entering the bedroom, and silence gave way to the sounds of the waking world. I could hear footsteps on the cobbles outside the hotel, and somewhere a girl was singing, and far up in the hills a farmer was shooting rabbits, and the sound of the shots was like someone knocking together blocks of wood in the stillness of the air. The light was growing. It began to flash and glitter, to assume shape and form, rising bodily from the sea. The pinewoods caught fire and turned to milky gold, and it seemed as though the veils of the sky were peeled away until at last there would be revealed the face of the naked heavens. The light came swirling up the thickly wooded hills, penetrating the dark and shape-less places, sending out filaments of silver and blue to explore the unknown misty heights, and there was no restlessness in this light, no abruptness, no harsh and jagged edges. Light smiles in France, and has the glow of healthy flesh. In Greece the light shouts, but in France it sings. In Greece, too, the light advances with a godlike tread, with a shaking of furious banners; in France it comes joyfully and quietly, like a woman entering a room.

So I thought, leaning out of the window and taking in great gulps of the sea-scented air, no longer aware that I was in Eze, for this view from the window was like a glimpse of a legendary coast un-touched by men, so dark, so blue, so mysteriously full of trembling lights. These virgin mornings, where the air is thrice-washed and thrice-blessed, must come as a shock to the traveler from New York, who rarely sees such radiance. When the light lapped the window, I dressed hurriedly and went out to walk through the streets of Eze before the morning traffic had begun.

It was still early, and the night's dews still moistened the cobble-stones. It was damp and dark between the high walls of the houses, which have hardly changed since the fifteenth century. The paths are steep; they climb, descend, turn in upon themselves, and they are rarely straight for more than ten yards, and all the houses are on different levels. Eze clings to its rock by virtue of providential mira-cles, but having grown accustomed to its miraculous existence over

the centuries, it wears a sophisticated air. The town claims to be the
oldest in France, deriving its name from the Egyptian goddess Isis,
whose bird is blazoned on its armorial bearings. Isis, Isiae, Eza, Heze,
Eze—it has had many names, and many conquerors. The Phoenicians
built a fortress on these heights, Roman legionaries marched through
its narrow streets, the Moors captured it and built its vaulted passage-
ways, and the Holy Roman Emperor annexed it. Once it belonged
to the kingdom of Lotharingia. We know that at some time in the
fifteenth century the castle on the summit was blown up with gunpowder, for there is still in existence a letter written by Amadeus VIII
of Savoy, dated 1407, saying how deeply he regretted the destruction
of his castle. The French revolutionaries captured the town from the
Italians, but the Italians claimed it again after Napoleon's defeat, holding it until 1860, when a plebiscite organized by Napoleon III and
Cavour left the town in the possession of France. But it is useless to
speak of history at Eze. There are few documents, and one might as
well attempt to compile a history of a pirate's lair. Mistral called it
"the eagle's nest"—*lou Nidou d'aigla*—and no one has ever improved
on this description. This small town is so high, so improbable, that it
seems to be outside history altogether.

In the early morning, walking through those dark streets, one has
the impression of embarking on a journey into a remote and nameless past. A Phoenician sailor, a Roman legionary, or a veiled Moorish
prophet would be more appropriate in this setting than a French girl
in swinging skirts. The familiar smell of French bread is faintly
shocking. The streets are dark, like the bottom of a well, and you
have to climb up to the curiously named *jardin exotique* on the very
pinnacle of the rock before you see the light again. There are almost
no sounds—no horses, no automobiles, no shop bells. The sea is far
away, and Eze dreams quietly on its pinnacle of rock.

Wandering through those streets is a little eerie. There is almost no
sense of contact with the real world. Nice and Villefranche and
Monaco are hardly more than ten minutes away by car, but you
would think you are a thousand miles away. There are three or four
vast palatial residences clinging perilously to the rock, but they are
hidden away behind high walls, and most of the residents live in

small, low buildings made of massive stones from the nearby mountains; the doors are very low, and small; and underneath these small houses are great honeycombed cellars which may have been tunneled by the ancient Gauls and Ligurians who once inhabited this rock. Even today you can walk for twenty minutes through the town without encountering anything more modern than a fifteenth-century well head carved in bronze.

But the glory of Eze is in the light, and I went back to my window at the *Chèvre d'Or*, named after the mysterious golden goat which is said to lie hidden in many places of southern France, waiting for the day when it will emerge in all the splendor of its virility. My friend Sevek, the painter, was waiting for me with steaming coffee and breadrolls, and over breakfast we set about discussing the quality of the light that poured through the wide-open windows. We had both traveled through the Middle East and could discuss learnedly the quality of the sunlight flowing down from the snow-capped Elburz Mountains onto the plain of Teheran: the most palpable light we had ever known. Then there were the floodlit golden noons of the Nile and the silver glow over the Greek islands and the purple light flowing steadily over Athens.

"It's a mysterious light," I said. "I don't know how one could describe it."

He peered out of the window, tasting the light, letting it wash over his eyeballs. As an artist he had spent most of his life wrestling with the sunlight, as Jacob wrestled with the angel. He painted in watercolors, which are free-flowing, not with oils, which are earthbound.

"It's the usual light," he said. "It is like this every morning. I don't know why people don't come here in crowds simply to enjoy the light, but I'm glad they don't. Eze is not fashionable yet, and I hope it never will be."

He laughed deep down in his throat.

"I've traveled all over the world, and never known a place like this," he went on. "There are days when I forget the big towns exist, and there is only Eze. I'm supremely happy here. I'll never leave. I'll stay here until I am old and bent. Do you know, this must be the only place in the world where you feel that the drawbridge has been pulled up, and you can be alone with yourself. Modern civilization stops at the gates of Eze, and that's best."

Sevek is Polish-Austrian, and from long acquaintance with France he has become more French than the French. He has a long dark face and melting dark eyes, and a curious way of hiding in himself to emerge suddenly and unexpectedly, as though springing out of a cave. He was talking about Eze and his beautiful French wife and the Madonna he had painted for the church, and then he said very quietly: "Look, the light is enjoying itself."

So it did, and there was no longer any need to search for the peculiar quality of the light which shines in the south of France, and never more splendidly than when it shines on the white walls of Eze.

I was haunted by Sevek's words as I went wandering over France, for they were like the simple melody which lies at the heart of a fugue, and endless variations and improvisations could be played on them. There was so much truth in the phrase that it explained much that was mysterious and concealed. I would think of this new and still unfamiliar concept of light enjoying itself as I walked among the foothills of the Pyrenees or wandered over ancient battlefields or looked out over the coast of Normandy from Mont-Saint-Michel, and it seemed to me that the pieces of the jigsaw puzzle were beginning to come together.

All through French history there has been this intense devotion to light, this quiet reveling in it. The light, the colors of the air, were for the French the purest joy, and they celebrated their joy in stained glass windows, in brilliantly colored books and dresses, in Impressionist painting, in a continuing debate on the nature of light, in endless speculations on its strange and exhilarating behavior, as though it were a living thing. Because the light was feminine, and desired to please and to be seen, they opened up the walls of their cathedrals to let it in, and because the light was self-conscious and determined to be shown in its utmost splendor, they filled the windows with those thousands of pieces of colored glass, as thin as wafers, which are the great glory of medieval France. Light spoke to them; it was the voice of angels. "In the name of the voice comes brightness," said Joan of

Arc mysteriously at her trial, and the inquisitors were puzzled. They might have been less puzzled if they had read the long discourses on the nature of the divine light written in the twelfth and thirteenth centuries in France, or even if they had read the strange little verses on the nature of light which the Abbot Suger carved on the first of all Gothic churches, having built his church as a proclamation of his faith in the divinity of light, in its perfect beauty. *"Au nom de la voix vient la clarté."* It is as though those words, uttered simply by an eighteen-year-old girl, were a banner floating high above France.

Lumière, lucidité, clarté—even now these are the words that work most strongly on the French imagination. France is the child of light, and there is a sense in which she is forever dedicated to Apollo, the god of the heavenly light. From this love of light comes clarity, and from clarity comes the clear intelligence, and the desire to reason, and that swift curving line which appears everywhere in French design. *Splendeur*, too, is a word they have made peculiarly their own. Originally it meant the reflection of the heavenly light, and was so used in theological treatises, but the French quite reasonably identified the heavenly and the earthly lights. France seems to hover between earth and heaven like the rainbow, whose colors fill her cathedrals.

But if we follow the French and attempt to employ reason and seek out the nature of this light, we find ourselves tongue-tied. The rich, fruitful, feminine quality of that light is too evident to need explanation. The light enjoys itself. It jumps and tumbles and floats and waves its scattered veils with a curious impudence. It smiles at its own reflection in the mirroring earth as a beautiful woman smiles in acknowledgment of her own beauty, but why this should be so— why it should be so caressing and playful—is a mystery beyond any man's understanding. We think of Paris as *la ville lumière*, and it is unthinkable that the word could be attached to London, Rome or even Athens. In the light that shines over France there is an extraordinary gentleness, and a desire to please, and all this we acknowledge without being able to explain it.

There are other and even stranger things which can be discovered from the rocky pinnacle of Eze. Standing on the summit of the rock, in that twenty yards of garden which it amuses them to call a *jardin exotique*, though there is nothing in the least exotic about it, you look down at the quiet shores with the sea so far below that even its ripples have melted into the distance. The garden is drenched in sunlight. The green cactuses are like little green bursts of fire. The white ruins of an ancient fortress blaze and shine, and the heavens pour down endless fountains of light, and all the coast is gentle as a dream, in the blue haze of summer. But turn north, and the beauty vanishes. Those ribbed and muscular mountains have a gauntness which is intimidating. Foreigners think of the south of France as a gentle country, but in reality it is harsh and fierce, and the ghosts linger. The march of the Roman legionaries has not completely crushed the memories of the ancient Ligurians and Gauls, and the rich who have their villas in the south of France are rarely aware how close they are to ancient savageries. The land is haunted. The ghosts put on flesh and walk in the remote villages, which are pagan still under a veneer of Christianity. The French intelligence does not derive only from the light; it comes too from the terrible rebelliousness in the French soul, a fierce exultation in their own powers. Too many races are mixed up in them—Phoenician, Greek, Roman, Gaul and Northmen—to enable them to live easily with themselves. Those heavy, brooding mountains in the south suggest undreamed-of ferocities. Danger lurks there, and sometimes it is better to turn away and look down on the quiet shores and the sunlit sea like D. H. Lawrence:

> *The sea will never die, neither will it ever grow old*
> *nor cease to be blue, nor in the dawn*
> *cease to lift up its hills*
> *and let the slim black ships of Dionysus come sailing in*
> *with grape-vines up the mast, and dolphins leaping.*

THE COMING OF
THE GREEKS

The Greeks came early to the land of France: how early, and by what sea roads we may never know. The first Greek settlers came probably from the island of Rhodes about 650 B.C., driving their long, lean ships around the coast of Italy and settling on the shores of the Rhône between Arles and the sea. They gave their own name to the river, which they called Rhodanos, and to the land all around, which is called Rhodanie to this day, and at the mouth of the river they built the towns of Rhodanusia and Heraclea, which have long since vanished. Today their settlements lie buried beneath the earth, and only a few scraps of Rhodian pottery and a few walls, like the great fortress wall discovered by Henri Rolland at Saint-Blaise on the Etang de Berre, remain to remind us of their ancient conquest. They vanished, but other Greeks came after them.

About 600 B.C. another wave of Greeks settled in southern France. They came from Phocaea, the northernmost of the Ionian cities on the western coast of Asia Minor. At this time the Phocaean fleet was the second most powerful in all the Mediterranean, rivaling the fleet of the Carthaginians. Hungry for colonies, they built great pente-conters—ships with fifty oars—and, being friendly with the powers which controlled the Strait of Messina, they poured into the western

Mediterranean and established colonies wherever they beached their ships. The islands fell into their hands. One after another Ischia, Sardinia, Corsica, Elba, Majorca, Minorca and Ibiza became Phocaean outposts. They settled on the coast of Spain, sailed through the Gates of Hercules and entered the Atlantic. The Rhodians built white temples to Apollo, the god of the sunlight. The Phocaeans built temples to his sister Artemis, the huntress.

The Greeks tell a pleasant story about the founding of Marseilles by the Phocaeans. They say that Aristarchê, a lady of Ephesus, had a dream in which Artemis spoke to her, saying: "Take one of the statues which are sacred to me, and join with the Phocaeans under their captain, Simos, and his son Protis, merchants, and sail with them to the new land." She immediately sought out the merchants and told them of her dream, and she accompanied them on their expedition to the west, taking with her the cult statue of Artemis of the Ephesians. At last they rounded a cape and entered a bay so cunningly hidden that it was discoverable only to sailors who had long known the sea, and within the bay was a perfect harbor of clear, deep water with firm rock all round and space for a hundred ships to ride at anchor. But curiously there were no other ships in sight, no towns, no fortresses. They landed, and went up into the bare hills, and there discovered that all this land was claimed by the Ligurian King Nannos, who at that very moment was preparing to choose a husband for his daughter Gyptis. According to the custom, all the young rulers of the neighboring towns would be invited to a feast, and at a certain moment Gyptis would be brought in, carrying in her right hand a chalice of pure water, which she would offer to the youth who found most favor in her eyes. The Phocaeans, as a mark of honor, were invited to attend the feast, and when the beautiful Gyptis entered the room where the men were feasting, she went immediately to Protis and gave him the chalice. Then Protis took the chalice and drank the pure water, while King Nannos applauded, saying: "This thing was done by the gods." For all this had been arranged long ago by the goddess Artemis.

Protis married Gyptis, and they were given the harbor of Massalia, now Marseilles, as a wedding present. Protis, the happy bridegroom, changed his name to Euxinos, meaning "the honored guest," while Gyptis changed her name to Aristoxena, meaning "the best of guests." Because Gyptis came of royal blood, she became co-ruler with her Greek husband of the harbor and the wild shores, and because Artemis was the guardian goddess of the land, and had directed the Greeks along their dangerous journey, and was responsible for the marriage, the whole of this strip of southern France was given over to her keeping.

All this had come about because Aristarchê, the lady of Ephesus, had dreamed in the temple, and therefore she too was given a position of power. She became the priestess of the shrine of Artemis built overlooking the harbor, and the statue brought from Greece was placed in the sacred precincts. This statue, or perhaps a Roman copy of it, survives to this day in a museum in Avignon.

Such is the story told by Strabo and others of the second conquest of the Greeks in France. We have no reason to doubt the story. Something very like this must have happened. Coins from Phocaea have been found, together with coins from half the Greek cities of Asia Minor, in and around Marseilles: they bear the figure of Artemis or a griffin, and sometimes there is a crab, the emblem of naval power, and the letter M. The Phocaeans established colonies along the coast, usually wherever there were deep harbors with sheltering islands, for Phocaea had a deep harbor and was sheltered by three islands. They founded Antipolis (Antibes) and Nicaea (Nice), and sailed up the Rhône to pour fresh blood into the Rhodian settlement at Arles, which then bore the lovely name of Therine. They traded in timber, cattle, honey, skins and fish, until the Carthaginians attacked them and then they fled for a few years, only to return when the danger was over. For nearly six hundred years Marseilles remained the most powerful Greek outpost in the western Mediterranean. So she remained until the Romans conquered her, and even then the people of Marseilles continued to speak Greek and worship Artemis, the sister of Apollo and goddess of the sun.

Today the Côte d'Azur still bears the indelible traces of the ancient Greeks. There are the carved stones in the museums, and an entire Greek city has recently been excavated at Glanon near Saint-Rémy-en-Provence. There is the Provençal language, which is still spoken, with its hundreds of Greek words. The Greeks brought to France the vine, the fig tree, the cherry tree, the chestnut and the olive, and they changed the face of the land by cultivating it in a way which would support so many fruits. Those gray gnarled olive trees, in their orderly rows, are the descendants of olive trees planted thousands of years ago.

The Greeks left their stamp on southern France in ways which are past counting. They brought with them the worship of the sun, and the sense of the gaiety of life. Artemis remained, and in time she would wear the crown of the Virgin Mary. The Greeks came open-handed, not as conquerors but as settlers, and they found in France the same clarity, the same silvery-golden light, they had known in Greece. It is said that the men of Marseilles found their wives in Arles. What is certain is that the women of Arles possess a particular beauty, very calm and grave and sweet, which is essentially Greek. They have wide foreheads, delicate chins and enormous eyes, and they laugh easily, but with a kind of gravity, as though even laughter were something to be tasted with exquisite pleasure. They are the most beautiful of all French women, and you will see the same faces on the Parthenon reliefs.

Not far from Arles, in the shadow of those fierce and tormented mountains called the Alpilles, an entire Greek city has been uncovered. Along the slopes of the mountains, far below the cornfields where Van Gogh once painted, stands the ancient Glanon, with its white courtyards and colonnades, and temples to Cybele, the Great Goddess, and to Atys, the shepherd boy who was her lover. Still in place are the bearded river gods from whose mouths the streams flow out of the mountain, and the altars ornamented with laurel wreaths and human ears which were dedicated to the voice of the goddess. The temple roofs have fallen in, and no houses have been left standing, but the baths and mosaics and marble benches have not changed since the Greeks wandered through these wide white streets and made their way up terraced steps to the sanctuary in the mountains. You can wander here for hours without setting foot outside a Greek city. Especially beautiful are the immense flaring *acroteria*, like sudden blazing bunches of flowers in terra cotta, with which the Greeks ornamented the roofs of their buildings. The *acroteria* of Glanon are the most delicate and the best preserved that have ever been found.

There was a time when Glanon was an important frontier city between the Greeks of Marseilles and the Gauls. Glanon coined its own money and imposed its own taxes. It was a political center, a market place, a trading post. Here rich merchants from Marseilles built their villas, for then as now the Alpilles protected the inhabitants from the full force of the mistral, that fierce and enervating wind which blows out of the north. Here there was water in abundance, and those who wanted stone had only to climb the mountain to get it.

For centuries the Greeks must have lived in peace with their neighbors, for we find Gauls living within the city walls, growing rich, building their own villas and acting as priests and priestesses in the temples. The Gauls seem to have lived there before the coming of the Greeks, for the statues of their tribal gods have been found, usually headless, and here too there have been found the curious niches in which the headhunting Gauls placed human heads. There are moments, especially at dusk, when the purple shadows hover over the white city, when you can easily imagine the Greeks emerging from their columned houses and sunning themselves in the little patches of sunlight that remain. In the museum at Saint-Rémy you will find the treasures of Glanon quietly and triumphantly displayed —the flaring *acroteria*, the sculptured reliefs, the three-horned bulls, the heads of Greek gods, the Roman empresses, the fruit of three cultures. There is a purely Greek simplicity, a Greek sense of form in the calm and undemonstrative museum, where the walls are white and the treasures gleam like jewels.

THE GREEN VASE

All the Greek treasure found in France pales before the splendor of a Greek vase. This beautiful and richly designed vase, of the finest Greek workmanship, was found in the small village of Vix near Châtillon-sur-Seine, a hundred miles southeast of Paris. The French themselves are a little in awe of this vase. No one has yet satisfactorily explained what it was doing so close to Paris. Was Paris also a Greek outpost?

Châtillon-sur-Seine is an inhumanly difficult place to get to. It is a famous town. Saint Bernard lived there. Marmont, Duke of Ragusa, was born there. It was General Joffre's headquarters in World War I, and here the armies of General Leclerc and General de Lattre de Tassigny joined forces in 1944. If you take the train from Paris to Troyes and then change to a branch line, it will take you twelve hours to reach Châtillon. I thought it might be simpler to go by way of Dijon. There the station master pointed out there were only two trains a week, and both started at four o'clock in the morning. Yes, Châtillon was an inhumanly difficult place to get to. He looked at the *horaire des trains* again, and smiled. "I must excuse myself, *monsieur*," he said. "Those trains that start at four o'clock in the morning only run in summer." It was October, and it looked as though the problem of reaching Châtillon would never be solved.

"Is there no other way?" I asked.

"No other way that I know," he replied. "Perhaps you might engage a taxi. It is about eighty kilometres away."

So I wandered into Dijon and wondered how much of the day would have to be spent in looking at Burgundian cathedrals, for which I have no fondness. There was a bus station near the railroad station. I asked whether there were any busses running to Châtillon. "There is one a day, *monsieur*, and it left five minutes ago."

But by a miracle the bus had been delayed, and I jumped on it just as it was setting out for Châtillon.

It was one of those bright, clear October days, the sky very high, the birds twittering, and all the Burgundian countryside stretching softly into the smoky blue distance. The bus was in no hurry. It stopped at every hamlet on the road, and instead of going due north it wandered as far as Is-sur-Tille in the east before backtracking through the gentle rolling country where the River Seine has its source. At each village the bus dropped off a sack of grain, or car springs, or a child's toy, and a packet of mail. There were long leisurely conversations between the handsome crewcut driver and the village girls. He was in good humor, and was perfectly content to drink an *apéritif* at every village on the road. About half the villages were named after the Seine, which is here no more than a thin winding stream. There were villages called Saint-Seine, Saint-Marc-sur-

Seine, Nod-sur-Seine, the last being the most appropriate. With sanctity and sleep as our companions we made our way through a smiling countryside.

Châtillon-sur-Seine proved to be a sleepy little town which had long ago forgotten its heroic past as a fortress and advance post of the Dukes of Burgundy. It had forgotten Marmont and Joffre and Leclerc and De Lattre de Tassigny, just as it had forgotten Garibaldi, who led an uprising here in 1870 against the Germans. Far more familiar to the town people was a nameless princess, of an unknown tribe, who in some remote and uncertain period of the past was buried nearby with gold treasure heaped beside her. This was treasure comparable with Schliemann's discoveries at Troy and Mycenae, and why it was buried near this town in northern France no one seemed to know. The shop windows were full of postcards depicting the treasure, or posters showing the great vase, which was once gleaming bronze but is now covered with a patina of the richest, the most luxuriant green.

Down the street from the bus station, beyond the bridge over the gently flowing Douix River, stands a Renaissance house which was bombed during the war, though it has been restored to its former magnificence. The house has been converted into a museum, and on the first floor is the treasure. You enter the room and you are immediately confronted with the green vase. It is no ordinary vase. Five and a half feet high, weighing nearly a quarter of a ton, a huge bellying thing of tremendous power and authority, dominating by its mere presence, this vase outshines everything else in the room, which is filled with gold and bronze vessels and diadems more ancient than any other treasure discovered in France. Around the rim of the vase march charioteers and soldiers in Corinthian helmets and short coats, otherwise naked, and horses carved so smoothly, with such quick, nervous, graceful and spirited bodies that they seem to belong more to our own time than to ancient Greece. The vase is Greek, either from the mainland or from the colonies in southern Italy, and it was clearly made at the ripest period of Greek art, before the Persian invasions.

Nothing quite like this vase has ever been brought to light before, and there is nothing comparable to it in Greece. There exist smaller vases of the same general shape, with figures carved around the rim, and handles shaped like gorgon heads, but none of them have this perfection, this kingly majesty. The greatest of them would hold three or four gallons of wine. This vase could hold over a thousand gallons. Staggering in its dimensions, sumptuous in its ornamentation, and in the rich contours of the bellying curve, it represents Greek art at the summit of perfection. All round this vase are the other objects found in the tomb—a massive gold diadem ornamented with miniature winged horses, bronze brooches, anklets, necklaces, ewers, wine jars, the remains of a sumptuously equipped funeral chariot—but it is the great vase which attracts and keeps your attention until its massive shape, suggesting fruit in superb ripeness, is indelibly imprinted on the mind.

Heaven knows how it ever came to this corner of France sometime in the sixth century B.C. Châtillon, they say, lies at what was once the highest navigable point of the Seine, whence there were portages to the Rhône. Ships laden with tin from England could make their way as far as Châtillon, and then their merchandise would be transferred to horse carts and taken to a river port on the Rhône, and so down the Rhône to the Mediterranean and the great seaports of Etruria, Greece, Egypt and North Africa. We know that tin left England in vast quantities, but we do not know the route it took on its southward journey; and no one has ever found in Châtillon even the smallest nugget of tin. Did Châtillon derive its wealth from a tax on tin? Was it a great trading center? Did this Celtic princess rule over a vast area of France? No one knows. All we know for certain is that someone died here, and was buried, and Greek treasure such as was offered only to great kings was heaped into the tomb. It would hardly be stranger if we found the body of an ancient Greek prince, with all his armor about him, in the Mojave Desert.

This treasure is more tantalizing than the treasure dug up by Schliemann. Such majestic vases were made very rarely in antiquity, and they are always associated with kings and queens of vast wealth. We know of similar vases which were offered to King Croesus of Lydia, to Queen Semiramis, and to Ptolemy Philadelphus; there are hardly any others. Such vases were emblems of power and majesty, and no one drank wine from them. Like crown jewels they were handed down from generation to generation, and they occupied a place of importance in the palace. Herodotus tells a strange story of a gigantic vase which the Spartans offered to King Croesus about the year 546 B.C. in return for the gifts the king had given them, which is perhaps only another way of saying that the vase was offered as an act of homage. King Croesus never received the vase, for it was already on its way to Sardis when he was attacked and made prisoner by the Persian King Cyrus, and soon the vase passed mysteriously into the possession of the islanders of Samos, who in turn offered it up to the goddess Hera, placing it in her shrine: for she was their guardian goddess. Here is Herodotus's story:

Accordingly the Spartans made an enormous vase of bronze, large enough to hold 300 *amphorae* and covered with figures of living creatures around the outside of the rim, and they sent this vase to Croesus in return for the presents he had given them, but for some reason or other it never reached the king. There are two quite different stories about the fate of the vase. One story says that somewhere off Samos the islanders got wind of its presence, put to sea in their warships and captured the prize; that at any rate is the story told by the Spartans. The Samians however tell another story, saying that the Spartans arrived too late, and hearing that Sardis had fallen and Croesus was a prisoner, they sold it to some citizens of Samos who placed it as an offering in the Temple of Hera. And indeed, if they sold it, it is likely enough that on their return to Sparta they would pretend they had been robbed by the Samians. So much for the story of the vase.

René Joffroy, the young schoolteacher and archeologist who was in charge of the excavations, has made the interesting suggestion that the vase of Châtillon may be the identical vase offered to King Croesus by the Spartans. It is not a wildly improbable suggestion, for the date of the vase cannot be far from 546 B.C. Moreover, the vase was found together with a lid crowned with a small statue which may very well have been added by the Samians to represent the goddess Hera. It is the statue of a veiled woman, of a style very different from the carving on the rest of the vase, giving every impression of being added later for a special occasion. Samos, which lies near the coast of Asia Minor, had a turbulent history, changing hands twenty times in two hundred years, and the very turbulence of its history suggests that the Samians may have founded colonies far from their islands, just as nearby Rhodes founded colonies in southern France.

So we may imagine some Samian prince escaping with the treasure during the height of the wars, landing in southern France and progressing northward along the valley of the Rhône until in the course of time he was able to establish himself at Châtillon, and at his death being buried with the great vase intended for King Croesus. The French quite naturally insist that a Celtic princess was buried there, but the evidence of the bones which have largely melted into the earth is insufficient to prove whether it was a man or woman, Greek or Celtic, and whether it was a man or a woman is scarcely important: it is more important to know whether the tomb, surrounded with Greek works of art, belonged to a Greek. For, if it did, then we shall have to recognize that the Greeks penetrated deeper into France than we ever knew or suspected.

Today the great vase with its gorgon head handles and frieze of naked warriors and charioteers reposes in the upper room of the museum at Châtillon, a thing of extraordinary power and beauty, of a deep sea-green color, in an almost perfect state of preservation. It is one of those discoveries which tend to shatter our preconceived notions of history. It is not only that nothing like it is known, but no one has any idea where to look for a companion to it. So it remains, superb and isolated, seeming to pulsate with mysterious energy as it stands on its small wooden pedestal, as high as a man.

I wanted to know more about the finding of the vase, and by good luck in the little village of Vix two or three miles from Châtillon I found the man who dug it out of the earth.

THE PEASANT

That afternoon the sky was soaring high, and there were only a few tatters of clouds racing across the Burgundian countryside. It was autumn, and the plowed land lay quiet under the sun.

To reach the small village of Vix you take a side road which reaches almost to the slopes of Mont Lassois, a small, wooded hill long known to archeologists to be the site of prehistoric communities, for thousands of shards belonging to the Bronze Age have been discovered there. There are perhaps ten houses in the village, and the largest of them, at the turning in the road, is owned by Maurice Moisson. He was working in the fields that afternoon, a tall, thin, sunburned man with the big hands and the look of *un bon paysan*. He wore the usual clothes of a farmer, a heavy blue shirt and blue trousers. He was about forty-five, gap-toothed, with a toothbrush mustache, and deepset dark eyes, and indeed his eyes were the most memorable thing about him, quick, dark and penetrating. He did not move heavily, as most French farmers do. He was lightweight, and moved easily, with something of a dancer's poise. His name means "harvest," and everything about him suggested the keen farmer devoted to his land. Like most farmers he spoke rapidly and well, with never a trace of hesitation.

The field where the treasure was found was only a long stone's throw from his house. The brown cows were grazing, and a black-and-white bird dog was gamboling among them, barking for no good reason unless it was the sheer joy of barking. I said I wanted to see the place where the treasure was found.

"It's over there," he said. "In the middle of that field, where the stones are."

It was a field of yellowish-gray earth, deeply scored by the plow, stretching for perhaps two acres. The field sloped a little, and in the middle there was a scattering of white stones, all carved and chipped by the plow, looking from a distance like a sprinkling of snow. We stood among those scattered stones which once, centuries ago, crowned the tumulus of a dead prince or princess. A fresh wind was blowing. As far as the eye could see there were only fields and rows of slender trees on the skyline. He kicked one of the white stones.

"This is where we found it," he said. "Just here, about nine feet down. If you'll bend down, you'll see there's a very slight change in the slope. I used to worry about those white stones and the dip in the earth—I thought there might be something here because these stones don't come from this region. I used to ask myself what those chips of stone were doing here, and who brought them, and why, but I never did anything about it until the early days of 1953. It was in

January, the weather freezing, snow on the ground, and I took it into my head to dig here. It wasn't long before I came on the rim of the big vase."

He lit a cigarette and gazed across the fields with a faintly perplexed expression.

"So I sent a message to Monsieur Joffroy, the archeologist, who has been digging on Mont Lassois for many years. He's a *brave type*, and he knows his way around. He brought two or three helpers, and we all started digging. We had a pump working. We were up to our waists in mud and dirt, and it was freezing, and we worked through the night sometimes. The B.B.C. heard about it, and they sent a camera crew to televise the digging. Some of the stones in the mortuary chamber were 125 kilograms—stones upon stones. And all the things we dug out were all covered in mud, not beautiful. They had to be cleaned before we could see how beautiful they were, and when I saw them later I could scarcely believe it.

"For thirty-two years, *monsieur*, I have been keeping my eyes open and looking for treasure. I've listened to the old men talking about the finds made here in the past. They found Greek treasure at Sainte Colombe only a few miles from here during the last century, and it's in the museum for everyone to see, but nothing compares with the treasure we found here. We keep looking. We have a feeling for the earth, and someday we may find some more, but another great vase— no, that's unlikely. Swords, pins, bracelets, shards, even a temple which we can trace through Roman and Merovingian times, but not a vase like this. This vase is something we never dreamed of."

I asked him what he thought he would discover when he started digging.

"I didn't have any idea—maybe some bracelets or an old sword. But when I saw those heavy stones under the ground, and realized they had been put there deliberately, then I knew it would be something important. I knew someone had been buried here, and I knew there would be treasure of a kind, but I never suspected there would be so much."

"If there was so much here," I suggested, "then perhaps all this field is a necropolis, and there is still more treasure to be found."

He shook his head sadly.

"No, we've dug across the field, but we never found anything else. Not a pin, not a sword blade. If you look over there on the horizon, between those trees, you can see a faint hump in the earth—they found bracelets there, but the tomb must have been rifled long ago. We have looked, *monsieur*. We have good eyes, but it seems there is nothing left in the earth."

It was strange to be standing there in the middle of a plowed field, knowing that the greatest of all Greek treasures discovered in France had been lying quietly underground for twenty-five centuries, and there was nothing to distinguish this field from a hundred thousand others except that barely perceptible dip and the scattering of stones which looked like so many marble chips. Less than half a mile away stood the frowning hill of Mont Lassois, which must have been a citadel at one time commanding all the plains around, and from the heights watchers must have gazed from the watch towers to look for the presence of ships coming up the Seine less than a mile away; and there were signal fires, and armed men, and the booths of traders and moneychangers, and stables for the horses, and temples and palaces, but all have gone. The small village of Vix may have been as important as Mycenae, but no poets sang about it, and its history will have to be pieced together from whatever is found in the earth. And I was puzzled that so little was being done. I would have thought the archeologists would flock here, and all the neighboring fields and all of Mont Lassois would have been honeycombed by now, for it is unlikely that there is not more treasure. Here, if anywhere, treasures are to be found.

As we walked across the darkening fields, where silvery threads of gossamer clung to the plowed earth, I asked him what he felt on that cold, blustery evening when his spade rang against the top of the great vase.

"Joy," he answered. "The purest joy imaginable. *Voyez-vous*, such things do not happen many times in the life of man."

"You'll find more treasures," I suggested.

"No, *monsieur*, we shall never find treasures like this again," he said sadly, and there was on his face the expression of a man who knows he has no more worlds to conquer. Over the years he would go on digging quietly, but never again would he see a great green vase and treasures of gold coming out of the ground.

It was dark when I took the bus back to Dijon. In these country places the darkness lies thick and heavy, with only a few small lights shining in the villages. As the bus sped along the winding roads, it was strange how every dark hill came to resemble an ancient tumulus.

THE HEADHUNTERS

The Gauls are a mysterious people, and when we think we have caught a glimpse of them they vanish in the mists of history. They stand like ghostly sentinels at the gates of France, a strange, erratic, courageous, brilliant people—how strange they were we are only beginning to know.

We do not know where they came from, whether they were tall or short, dark or fair, blue-eyed or dark-eyed. They left no literature, and only a handful of their words have survived. We know little about their marriage customs and still less about their system of land tenure. They seem to have lived peacefully with the Greeks who settled in the south of France, for they borrowed the Greek alphabet and modeled their coins on Greek originals. They had a sense of violent design, for in their hands the gold staters of Alexander the Great became formidable abstract designs. The Greek geographer Strabo, writing about the time of Christ, describes them as "war-mad, high-spirited and eager for battle, though otherwise simple and not unmannered." He thought them simple-minded because they would rush to battle at the first sign of alarm, and employed no feints or stratagems. They were the inventors of the *levée-en-masse*.

Until very recently we never saw the Gauls as they saw themselves. What little information we possessed came from Strabo, Julius Caesar and a few sculptured monuments. We know from sculptures on the triumphal arch at Orange that they fought naked, with long, narrow shields, and wore their hair like Hindus with a looped knot at the top of their heads, and they shaved off their beards and cultivated long mustaches. From other sources we know that they had a fondness for bleaching their hair, and like the Greeks they were perpetually washing themselves with soap, and they wore shoes with wooden soles which the Romans called *gallicae*. Their women were proud and independent, nearly equal to the men in the social community. They lived in primitive wooden cabins daubed with clay. They were excellent boat builders, leather workers, road makers and iron miners, and they were credited with the invention of the wooden wine barrel: on one famous occasion they filled wine barrels with inflammable material and rolled them down on a Roman army. Caesar pointed out that their chief characteristics were *nobilitas, levitas* and *infirmitas animi,* by which he meant that they were aristocratic, lighthearted and incapable of sustained effort. It has been contended that the modern French suffer from the same characteristics, and while it is true that they are lighthearted and betray a tendency toward aristocratic behavior, it would be dangerous to accuse them of being incapable of sustained effort. Posidonius, the Greek historian, writing about the time of the final defeat of the Gallic empire, speaks of their quick intelligence and exceptional powers of understanding.

Caesar tells us nearly all we know about their social and religious customs. He tells us that they measured the time not by days, but by nights, but offers no explanation for this strange reversal of a normal custom. He speaks of their many gods: Mercury, the pathfinder and inventor of crafts, Apollo, Mars, Juno and Minerva, calling them by their Roman names because their gods had the same qualities as the Roman gods, and it is significant that he placed Mercury first. We know the names of about four hundred Gallic gods, for the names changed over the length and breadth of Gaul. To Mars were dedicated the spoils of war, and anyone who kept any of the spoils for himself was tortured to death. Before a war they sacrificed human victims, and even during times of peace there were frequent sacrifices. Huge wickerwork baskets shaped roughly to resemble a human body were erected, and into these were poured malefactors of all kinds. Then the wicker baskets were set on fire.

The Romans were just as cruel, but their cruelty never extended to making these enormous wicker baskets filled with perhaps twenty men, some in the legs, some lying along the arms, some forming the body and the head, and all burning together. It is a refinement of spectacular cruelty which seems to have been peculiarly Gallic. Caesar noted that they cremated their dead, throwing into the flames everything the dead man was fond of, including his animals; and sometimes slaves and members of his family were thrown into the flames. If a chieftain died, his wife and whole family might be tortured to death if there was the slightest suspicion cast on them. Found guilty, they would be burned at the stake.

Caesar portrayed the Gauls as an intense, priest-ridden, mechanically-minded people, quick to copy Roman fashions in armaments, capable of astonishing acts of daring, brilliantly led, but rarely capable of unity, for they consisted of innumerable tribes each led by an independent king whose chief task was to preserve his autonomy. Caesar speaks approvingly of the vast power enjoyed by the priests. They officiated at all ceremonies, ordered all sacrifices, sat in judgment over all legal cases, and formed a close-knit group of spiritual chieftains whose power was quite as great as that of the nobles. They alone knew the contents of the sacred books, and they alone had the gift of prophecy. They believed in the transmigration of souls, and they taught this doctrine to the soldiers, who were therefore unafraid of death. Caesar believed that their doctrines all came from Britain.

The features of the Gallic gods, as they have come down to us, show extraordinary power. They are not gods to be trifled with. They are shown as thickset, heavy men, nearly always bearded, with blazing, deepset eyes, usually depicted in attitudes of violent movement. We see them on those strange altar stones which were unearthed in 1711 by workmen digging a burial crypt for the archbishops of Paris under Nôtre Dame: the stones are preserved at the Cluny Museum. One of these altar stones dates from the time of Tiberius and bears the first known reference to the Parisians. It reads: TIB CAESARE AVG IOVI OPTVM MAXSVMO S NAUTAE PARISIACI PVBLICE POSIERVNT. *In the time of Tiberius Caesar Augustus the sailors of Paris publicly raised this altar to sacred Jove, the great and the good.* On other altar stones we find Esus, the Gallic god of summer, half-naked and ferocious, with a sickle in his hand, about to cut down the sprig of sacred mistletoe. He was the god of workers and sailors who required muscle in their toil, a haunter of the woodlands, the possessor of the power of the ancient oak trees, an insatiable demander of sacrifices, for it was in his name that men were nailed to the forest oaks and sometimes burned on oak pyres. On another altar stone there is the equally fierce portrait of Cernunnos, "the horned one," who wears the horns of a deer or a ram, and is usually depicted sitting crosslegged like a Buddha. As Esus was originally the god of the forests—those forests which stretched across the whole of Gaul—so Cernunnos was the god of cattle and all horned animals, and of the moon, and of death. There were two-headed gods, and there were goddesses who lived in the streams or in strange rocks and in the clefts of the mountains. The pantheon of the Gallic gods was becoming unmanageable at the time of the Roman conquest.

All this, and much more, has been known about the Gauls for a long time, but it was only recently that we learned that they were headhunters. Like the Dyaks of Borneo they kept smoked heads in their houses, and whole collections of heads were made by the chieftains, to celebrate their victories.

Posidonius had written long ago that they were headhunters, but no one had believed it. The heads had perished: there was no evidence to support an ancient Greek historian who wrote that they nailed the heads to the doors of their houses or carried them suspended on a chain from their necks. Caesar, though he spent his best years campaigning in Gaul, had failed to note this propensity of theirs. Then quite suddenly, with the discovery of the Gallic *oppidum* at Entremont, a few hundred yards from Cézanne's studio on the hills overlooking Aix-en-Provence, the evidence of headhunting became overwhelming.

One afternoon I went to visit Cézanne's studio on the Chemin de Lauves, which the painter built during the last years of his life. It is now kept as a memorial to him, and an attempt has been made to show it exactly as it was. The house is solidly built, and the enormous studio downstairs is a pleasant place to linger in, wonderfully calculated to give a feeling of Cézanne's presence. Only one thing bothered me. Along a shelf there was a row of brown and decaying skulls. There were seven of these grinning skulls. Why so many? Why was he always painting them? What was the fascination he found in them? The presence of the skulls came as a shock. There they were, sitting like brown, overripe apples on a shelf, and there was no explanation for them. I left the studio, and walked up the winding road to Entremont.

It was one of those bright and blustery days with a gale blowing and the trees whistling in the wind. It was a steep climb among the pines, and I followed the path on the map. The path led to the gates of a naval radio station, and this was vaguely disturbing. There was no one in sight from whom I could ask directions.

As I climbed the hill, I recapitulated what little I knew about Entremont. Once, many years before Caesar's conquest of Gaul, there had been on this hill a great city, the capital of all the Gallic tribes of southern France whose territories reached from the Alps to the Durance. The tribes had formed a federation, and they had elected a king, Teutomalius, who ruled from this fortress city. Here were the temples and sanctuaries of the Gauls, their sacred writings, their best soldiers, with the king's palace and the great temple on the summit of the hill, while the tribesmen lived on the slopes. In 124 B.C. the armies of Teutomalius sacked Marseilles, which was under Roman protection. In the following year the consul Gaius Sextius Calvinus led an army against the sacred city of the Gauls, broke through the defenses with the aid of catapults, and sacked it. Teutomalius fled with a remnant of his forces, while the rest of the defenders were butchered or sold into slavery. The Roman general ordered the complete destruction of the city. The walls were leveled to the ground, the temples were defiled, the statues of the gods were broken up. Soon nothing was left of the white city on the hill, and its stones were used to build the fortified town of Aquae Sextiae, "the waters of Sextius," in the plain below. From Aquae Sextiae we derive the name of Aix.

I knew there were excavations there, and that part of the sanctuary had been unearthed, and this was all I knew. I had not expected to find a naval signal station on the top of the hill, with no sign of excavations anywhere. The signal station was surrounded by barbed wire, but the gate had been left open: there were radio masts, four or five quonset huts, a French flag fluttering from a high pole, and a heavy, repetitive thumping sound came from a gasoline engine. There were notices saying: KEEP OUT, with a skull and crossbones painted on them, but there was no one in sight. And still the gale was blowing and the trees were creaking, and from Aix below came faint voices on the summer wind. I was looking for ruins, but there seemed to be nothing but an abandoned signal station in a strange stormy light.

According to the map this hill was Entremont. In fact it was a signal station, and at any moment someone would emerge from one of the quonset huts and there would be trouble. Meanwhile there was only the brooding sense of emptiness and desolation under the lowering sky.

I was beginning to wish I was back in Cézanne's studio when a sailor swung out of the quonset huts and shouted something I could not understand, which I later realized was *"Défendu! Défendu!"* in a voice like a peal of thunder. He was red-faced, and gloriously angry.

"What are you doing here?" he roared at the top of his voice.

I said something about the excavations, and he kept roaring *"Défendu!"* until I thought he would burst.

When he was calmer, he said: *"Primo,* you are not allowed here! *Secundo,* you are not allowed to see the excavations. They are closed for the season."

He was imitating a machine gun and enjoying himself, but relented a little later, saying: "I'll show you the ditch. Remember, I could have you shot for coming here."

We walked past the hut where the gasoline engine was throbbing, up to a barbed-wire fence, and there five feet below the level of the ground lay an acre of excavations. At first sight it was not very impressive. For months afterward I was to dream of that poor, desolate little acre crowded onto the edge of the hill, but I confess the first impression was one of resentment. It was such a ludicrously small patch of earth and stones. People in Paris had spoken of Entremont with almost bated breath, saying that the archeological discoveries had opened a new page in the history of Gaul. There was very little to see. It looked as though some amateur archeologists had been at work. They had uncovered a few low walls, no more than two feet high, and there were hardly more than twenty of these walls in a space little larger than a garden. One could make out the shapes of small square houses—they must have been uncomfortably small—and there was a narrow stone-paved path running between them. Pine trees ran along the edge of the hill, and through the pines, where the hill curved down, one could make out some larger and heavier walls, but these were hardly more impressive than the white stones littered in the foreground.

"Is that all?" I asked.

"Yes, that's all. Now get out of here!"

For some reason he accompanied me to the open gate, laughing like a jovial storm trooper. The gale was increasing in fury, and the purple shadows were flinging themselves against the hill where the French flag on the high pole cracked in the wind.

We were ten yards from the gate when he gripped me by the shoulder and for the twentieth time explained that he had a perfect right to shoot me. Then he began to complain bitterly about the archeologists. For some time they had been trying to take possession of the whole hill. Who did they think they were? They were pompous little piss bodies, with no respect for the people who worked on the radio station. He had watched them at work as they crouched beside those low walls, sifting through mud and rubble, examining every stone, behaving like a crowd of old women. It was his opinion that they were up to no good, and for two pins he would knock down their walls. The truth was that they had been a nuisance to the radio station from the beginning. He gave me a shove, and said he hoped he would never see me again, and then I went through the open gate.

Halfway down the hill, I decided to go back. I had an odd feeling that I had missed something of importance—surely those pathetic little walls were not the only fruits of the excavators. Also, I was annoyed that the sailor should have the last word. I turned off the road, followed a long line of barbed wire, and crawled up through the walls

to the site of the excavation. The excavations were no more impressive than they had been the first time—the low, gleaming white stones
arranged in neat squares and the path running through them. There
was a notice saying it was forbidden to enter the site of the excavations under penalty of arrest.

I was about to leave when I saw something which made me catch
my breath. On one of the low hearthstones ten skulls had been
roughly incised. There were six small skulls, and four large ones, all
lying on their sides, and four paces beyond the hearthstone was
another upright stone showing a single skull with two hollows beside
it, each hollow large enough to hold a real skull, and there was no
doubt at all that this was the purpose of the hollows. This was perhaps
the stone of sacrifice, for it stood in the middle of the largest building
on the hill. There was an alarming gauntness and severity about it.
I wandered among the ruins, and found no more skulls. The fortress
walls were powerful, and evidently they encircled the hill; they were
ten feet thick in places. The excavation site, now that I was in it,
seemed smaller than before. The archeologists had been allowed to
dig on perhaps one-tenth of the summit of the hill, while the radio
station continued to operate on the remaining nine-tenths.

That was all, but it was enough. Those eleven skulls carved so
roughly into the stone—pear-shaped outline, slits for the eyes, nose
and mouth, nothing more—were strangely disturbing. They had the
crudity of naked power. If the naked Dyaks had carved them in the
forests of Borneo, one would not have been surprised, but it was
bewildering to find them in the south of France. Writing of the
people who once lived on this hill a Roman poet, Rufus Festus
Avienus, who lived in the fourth century A.D., when the memory
of these tribesmen was already fading, said: "There were once savages
here." So they were, and the eleven skulls were the evidence of their
savagery. The ghosts of a dead city were beginning to come to life
as I went down the hill.

The sailor complained about the archeologists, while in the museum
at Aix, where most of the discoveries at Entremont were housed,
there were complaints against the naval signal station, which apparently refused to permit the archeologists to dig over the hill.

"All we have been able to uncover," I was told, "is a very small part of the city. Luckily, we have found the sanctuary and the sacred way and an unexpectedly large number of statues, but there's no doubt that the whole of the top of the hill is full of Gallic remains. We have the money to dig, but everything is held up by the authorities in charge of the signal station. Yet in all of France there is no richer source for our knowledge of ancient Gaul."

The statues in the museum are impressive evidence that a hitherto unknown culture is coming to light. Those Gallic statues are heavy, roughly carved, curiously unattractive at first sight, but they grow on you. Power streams from them. The sculptors have seen Greek statues: they knew how to carve a body, a face, an arm, a shoulder, but they were unable to fuse them into a complete and satisfying whole. These statues are not intended to please, nor perhaps are they intended to strike the observer with fear. The emotion is tribal, earthy, fluid like lava. Five widely spaced fingers hold a decapitated head in their grasp. Sunk deep in stone is the face of a dead man vacant of all expression, except horror. An enormous warrior, wearing a tightly fitting leather coat with a medallion of a lion's head on his breast, sits cross-legged, serene and impassive, a thunderbolt in one hand, a skull in the other. There is a relief showing a chieftain riding on horseback, the skull of an enemy dangling between the horse's legs. Always the skull; always death. And that heaviness in the representation of the dead heroes ends by becoming completely convincing: those haggard faces have a strange power to charm. They convey authenticity. There is no attempt to make them pretty. They speak of a ruthless, unyielding, aristocratic people, half in love with death, with no hope of a future world, trusting in their own strength as long as their strength lasts. Long ago Posidonius, who had perhaps visited the capital of the southern Gauls at Entremont, for we know that he lived at Marseilles, commented that the sight of the skulls hanging in the houses of the chieftains had terrified him at first, but later he grew accustomed to them. So it is with these sculptures arranged on the ground floor of the Musée Granet at Aix-en-Provence. They are terrifying, as paintings of the Crucifixion are terrifying, but we grow accustomed to them.

"They hung the heads in their houses as though they were hunting trophies," wrote Posidonius, and perhaps they did, but trophy hunting was hardly their only purpose. It is more likely that they hung the heads for religious reasons in the belief that the *mana* of the dead had power to replenish the vital forces of the living.

Among the heads found at Entremont are some portraits of chieftains and heroes. For the first time we are able to see the Gauls as they saw themselves, with their long faces, high cheekbones, deepset eyes, and expressions of commanding severity. They are always tight-lipped and authoritative; there is not the ghost of a smile. One wears a diadem, another wears what appears to be a close-fitting leather cap with ear flaps. Both have the look of men accustomed to giving orders. There is a portrait of a veiled woman, and her expression is as severe as the expression of the men. Caesar spoke of their *levitas*, but no one would guess at levity by looking at the sculptures. Surprisingly, many of the heads resemble types which can be found in France today. Once when a head was being excavated one of the workmen shouted: "Napoleon!" There is another head with a remarkable resemblance to the French actor Louis Jouvet.

All these sculptures have been discovered since the Second World War. Very occasionally in the past, and always by accident, similar heads had come to light. In 1817 some seminary students wandering through Entremont discovered some death's heads carved in faint relief on stone. They took them back to Aix, but no one could offer any explanations. Eighteen years later, Prosper Mérimée, the Inspector-General of Ancient Monuments, better known as the author of *Carmen*, passed through Aix and was shown the strange stone. He wrote in his diary: "It seems to me it must be the work of the Salluvii, for only they could have done it so badly." The Salluvii were the chief tribe living on the hill, but more than a hundred years passed before Mérimée's guess was proved correct.

The first great discovery was made in 1943 by Germans who had established a radio station on the hill. Digging for a well, they found four mutilated heads and some fragments of statues. A few days later more fragments were found. News of the discoveries reached the French archeologist Fernand Benoît, who immediately realized their importance and began to wage his own war against the Germans in order to keep the discoveries in France, for the Germans tended to regard these sculptures as their personal possessions. Benoît succeeded in keeping the sculptures in France and organized a comprehensive excavation of the hill as soon as the Germans left, only to find himself engaged in a long and tiresome battle with the radio station. He uncovered the thick fortress walls and traced the course of the sacred way and the general plan of the sanctuary, where besides the statues of the gods and warrior princes he found human skulls. One had a ten-inch nail driven through it and had evidently stood within the sanctuary walls, while others had holes which permitted them to be carried on strings round the neck of the conqueror.

Years ago I used to find myself wondering at the curious feeling of the French for the human head. There are the innumerable heads which appear on the capitals of Romanesque churches, there is the invention of the guillotine, which can be seen now as the survival of an ancient and forgotten practice, and there is the traditional French insistence on the head rather than the heart as the seat of the soul. There is a sense in which the Greeks invented the human body, the Italians invented the torso, and the French the head as a work of art. When the poet Paul Valéry set out to write a brief history of a modern Leonardo da Vinci, he found an appropriate name ready and waiting for him—he called him Monsieur Teste, or Monsieur Head. It would not have occurred to an Italian or an Englishman to give him this name, but to Paul Valéry it was perfectly natural. To the French the head is the supreme work of art, the source of all intelligence, the soul's covering, the fountain of power. So across the centuries the intellectualism of Valéry finds a strange conformity with the headhunting Gauls.

A storm was coming up when I left Entremont at last. There were blue and white gashes in the purple sky, and the pines were creaking in the hot wind coming across the plains. The storm broke when I reached Aix and looked back to see the mysterious hill shining white in the lightning flashes. The clouds roared across the sky and in mid-afternoon the town was in darkness, and no street lamps were lit. It was like being back among the ancient Gauls.

THE ROMAN TRIUMPH

The Greeks came, and the Gauls, but they left only scattered traces which still work upon the feelings and the imaginations of the French. The Romans came like thunder and left indelible traces.

Littered all over southern France from the Italian coast to the Pyrenees are the visible remnants of the Roman conquest, which endured for four centuries. The Romans came in the full tide of power, hard-muscled and inflexible, determined to impose their own sense of order on the high-spirited, anarchic and aristocratic Gauls. They did nothing small. The Roman ruins are always vast, covering acres upon acres of ground. The huge arenas at Nîmes and Arles, the theaters at Orange and Vienne, the aqueduct called the Pont du Gard, even the Maison Carrée impress by their sheer size. They were not colonizers like the Greeks but conquerors aware of the majesty of conquest and their determination to retain all the fruits of conquest not for a few centuries but forever. They came to stay.

The Romans themselves had no doubt that they had come to stay, and they said as much in the memorials and inscriptions carved in bronze and stone across the length and breadth of France. The themes are always the same—the immensity of Roman power, the absolute subjugation of the tribes, whose names are listed at formidable length, each name representing an entire nation which has been annihilated or reduced to slavery. *"Sub imperium populi Romani redactae,"* reads the fearful formula. "Subjected to the authority of the Roman people." It was an evasive formula, for the Roman people were rarely consulted. Gaul became the private province of the Roman dictator.

The rule of the Romans in Gaul was strangely impersonal. These designers of immense roads and huge aqueducts, of towering arenas and vast theaters, seem to be faceless. We are rarely permitted a close view: their faces are in shadow, or masked, or hidden beneath the visors of their bronze helmets. They must have intermarried with the Gauls, and sometimes they must have shown signs of humanity, but we would never guess it from the surviving sculptures. They seem to be endlessly marching along the roads built by slave labor, endlessly uttering commands and erecting monuments to themselves; and at the first sign of muttering or revolt they swooped down on the offending village and put the villagers to the sword. Everything they built was heavy, harsh, sharp-edged and geometrical.

So it is at Nîmes, where the great arena, which could hold twenty-two thousand people, somehow suggests the abstract portrait of the Roman lieutenant-governor of the province. Coming upon the arena at night when it is brilliantly floodlit, it is almost impossible to avoid the impression that it is a magnificent portrait of a faceless man, massive, solid, unornamented, strangely inert. Few buildings are dead. Even a ruin will usually suggest the quivering life which went to the making of it. But the arena at Nîmes is grotesquely dead; there are only the white bones, the empty eyes of the arched windows gazing silently and impassively at the sky. It has the torpor, the weariness, the cruelty of death.

In daylight, under the blazing Mediterranean sky, the arena is even more disquieting. It has a gray-white ugliness, the stone is continually flaking away and forming little mounds of dustlike droppings, and there is the sense of impending doom. The sun beats mercilessly off the jagged stairways. For a moment you find yourself thinking you are caught in a vast prison. Standing at the center of the arena you feel like a wounded fly at the bottom of a cup. There is no escape, no way of surmounting those vast, mechanical walls with their rows of empty seats. At this moment you know what it is like to have been a gladiator—the enormity of it, and the horror.

The chief purpose of the arena at Nîmes was the exhibition of gladiators. Countless thousands of them died here, but only a handful of their names have survived. As they fought, fifty thousand eyes peered down at them, lusting for the sight of blood. Lost in the immensity of the arena the gladiators must have felt like insects. From end to end there was only a vast sea of sand. Encircled by a mindless wall of eyes, the gladiator could only turn upon his adversary with the fury of despair.

The arena was purely and simply an engine of destruction. Everything about its shape, its height, its dimensions speaks of the pointless death of some solitary individual lost at the bottom of a great curving cup of stone. Prisons, to be effective, should be round. The gladiator at the bottom of the pit at Nîmes might have died even more frightfully if he had had no adversary and no weapons. He would have died in paroxysms of terror at the sight of the circle of innumerable eyes desiring his death.

The arena is not a pleasant place. It is haunted by the ghosts of the dead gladiators, whose tombs, rudely carved, can be found in the local museum. The saddest of all is perhaps the tomb to the *retiarius* Lucius Pompeius, who fought armed with only a net and a short sword, and died at the age of twenty-five after winning nine victories. At the bottom of the tombstone are the words OPTATA CONIVX— *Optata, his wife*. It must have been a name he had given her, for it means "the desired one." This is all we shall ever know of Lucius Pompeius except that he was born in Vienne, the Roman capital of Gaul.

The full might of Roman power can be felt in Nîmes. The arena, the Maison Carrée, the Tour Magne, the Pont du Gard, a host of recently discovered mosaics all speak of imperious power employed with a kind of mechanical ruthlessness. The Roman city seems to have been founded by Augustus Caesar shortly after the conquest of Egypt, for its insignia is a crocodile chained to a palm tree. The crocodile has an iron collar round its neck.

At Vienne, perhaps because it was the capital of Gaul, the weight of Roman power seems to have fallen more lightly. There is a charming theater tumbling down the side of a mountain, and an unpretentious temple erected "to Rome and Augustus, son of the divine Caesar." The temple is gray with age, and has a look of quiet dignity and permanence. The Maison Carrée at Nîmes is irritating, dainty and commonplace, like an enormous ornate casket. The temple to Rome and Augustus seems to hug the earth and even now preserves a sense of ancient mysteries performed within the shuttered gates. At Vienne, too, there was an enormous circus fifteen hundred feet long, of which only the obelisk indicating where the chariots must turn remains. For centuries it pleased the people of Vienne to believe that the obelisk was the tomb of Pontius Pilate, thought to have been exiled to this city on the banks of the Rhône.

"Vienne the beautiful," wrote the Roman poet Martial, and so it remains. It was one of the few cities which revolted successfully against the Romans, and it has had a turbulent history ever since. After the revolt, the Romans simply went farther up the Rhône and founded the city of Lyons, but later they moved back to Vienne again, making it the headquarters of their fleet and giving it a new forum, a circus and a theater, for all of these were built during the later years of the empire. In Roman times Vienne was famous for its cloth; it still is. Today Vienne is a quiet backwater, but in Roman times it was the largest city in Gaul, with marble palaces facing the Rhône, and there were more palaces on the other side of the river.

Because Vienne was the capital of Gaul, innumerable Roman emperors passed through its gates, and when they were in danger they sometimes took refuge in this heavily fortified city. Among those who took refuge was the young and handsome Valentinian II. He had large soft eyes, high cheekbones, a petulant mouth. He was a prince from a fairy tale, full of generosity and an impatient desire to please. The chief of his imperial guard was a Frank called Arbogast, who seems to have been as evil as his name. Arbogast usurped the imperial power; he signed documents, or forced Valentinian to sign them; he bent the boy emperor to his will. Once when a man called Harmonius, accused of taking bribes, ran to the emperor for protection and concealed himself in the folds of the emperor's purple gown, Arbogast simply ran a sword through the gown. On another occasion, taunted beyond measure by the chief of his imperial guard, Valentinian unsheathed his sword. Arbogast laughed in the emperor's face. "Why draw your sword?" he asked. "Do you think you have the courage to kill me?" The emperor sighed: "I have not even the courage to kill myself."

Valentinian had powerful friends, and the most powerful was the saintly Bishop Ambrose of Milan. Milan was the capital of the Roman Empire, and Ambrose a lord temporal as well as the spiritual ruler of the capital. To Ambrose, Valentinian sent smuggled letters begging for help. Ambrose promised help, but it came too late. One day, while he was sleeping in one of his hunting lodges on the banks of the Rhône near Vienne, Valentinian was smothered to death, and then hanged, Arbogast apparently desiring to give the impression that the emperor had hanged himself. The emperor was scarcely twenty years old when he died.

The power and importance of Vienne increased under the Christian emperors. Then, from being the capital of Gaul, it became the capital of Burgundy and later of Provence. The Archbishop of Vienne bore the title of Primate of Primates over the Gauls, and magnificent processions streamed down the steps of the Cathedral of Saint Maurice, which looks out upon the Rhône. Then, as the years passed, the city sank into obscurity. Forgotten were the Roman emperors and the Christian martyrs who had brought it fame, for under Diocletian the streets had run with blood. The stones of the forum, the theater and the circus were used to build houses in the Middle Ages, and all the evidence of the Roman occupation vanished. Vienne slept its long sleep, becoming typical of those provincial cities which Balzac excoriated in his novels. Occasionally there would be a ripple of life, a spark, a flash, then the ripple would vanish and the spark would die out. There were riots in the cotton mills and a remarkable woman revolutionary emerged from obscurity to hold the stage for a moment, and then there was quietness again. Today Vienne is chiefly famous for the restaurant called *La Pyramide* which stands within the ancient circus.

We can tell how great Vienne must have been from a remarkable bronze head representing the titular goddess of the city which was found in the last century during some excavations. The goddess wears a crown marked COLONIA JULIA VIENNA, but the crown tells us less than her expression, full of power and dignity and a grave beauty. Once precious stones were inserted in the eye sockets, but even without her eyes she has a commanding aspect; and indeed the heavy lids and the mysterious darkness of her gaze only add to her beauty. She belongs to the first century A.D., for she wears her hair in heavy waves according to the fashion of that time. Curls escape over the nape of her neck and over her broad forehead. An extraordinary ripeness fills that face. The nose is long and straight, the upper lip small, the full lips are delicately modeled, and the chin is rounded and a little heavy, as fruit is heavy when it is ripening.

This goddess of Vienne betrays the influence of three cultures, for there is a Greek nobility in the design and a Roman sense of authority, while the workmanship—the way the bronze is hammered into shape— is essentially Gallic. She is a creature of changing moods. Seen in profile or three-quarter face she is all tenderness and grace; seen full face she exerts her authority to the full. As titular goddess of Vienne she ruled over a city which commanded the main road leading out of northern Italy from the Alps and over the Rhône, and the bronze head shows her perfectly aware of her power.

But what is even more extraordinary about her is her Frenchness. She could not have come from anywhere else but France. She represents a type which has endured over the centuries completely unchanged. Proud, volatile, forceful, she seems to belong to the earth and the heavens, human and divine. In some mysterious way she is at home in the world of the flesh and the world of the spirit.

The goddess of Vienne is a thing to wonder at, but there is another goddess in Toulouse who is almost as startling. The Musée Saint Raymond at Toulouse, opposite Saint Sernin, is not one of the great museums of France and cannot compare with the vast Musée des Augustins. A good deal of the museum consists of Roman sculptured heads, all of them lacking noses; its most notable possession is a collection of massive gold torques found in the village of Fenouillet in the Haute-Garonne, and these heavy gold ornaments have a truly barbaric splendor as they seem to quiver and coil like gold serpents, still alive although three thousand years have passed since they were fashioned. But the chief treasure of the Musée Saint Raymond is hidden in the shadows, and covered with a thick layer of dust: one could easily pass it and fail to notice that a singular work of art lay concealed there under the stairs, in that gloom which seems to hover over nearly all the provincial museums.

There is a sense in which this goddess of Toulouse is comparable to the superb goddess of Vienne, for both speak straight to the heart and were made by great craftsmen, and they tell us a good deal about the character of these ancient inhabitants of France. COLONIA JULIA VIENNA is all nobility and fire, but the marine goddess represented on the mosaic in Toulouse is sweetness and charm, smiling provocatively with her head inclined, naked and beguiling. She wears a scarlet cape which seems to be attached to her necklace and is in danger of falling away: only a small fragment of the cape rests on her right shoulder. Above her head, framing her, there is a kind of scalloped curtain in rainbow colors representing the waves of the sea, and she is holding the two ends of the curtain as though it were some kind of skipping-rope, so that we have the impression that she is about to jump out of the mosaic altogether. The mosaic is quite small, no more than two or three feet high, but even in its dust-covered state with all the bright colors muted, it is full of life and movement. There is not a hard line anywhere. She is all slender curves, and her head is a wheel of color giving movement to the rest. Consciously or unconsciously the artist designed her in terms of wheels within wheels— the wheel of the curtain, the wheel of her face, the half-wheel of the necklace, the great wheels of her breasts and the slender wheels of her shoulders, and there is even a wheel-like jewel hanging from her necklace. Perhaps it is from all these wheeling motions that we derive the feeling of an instinctive life moving within her. Under her heavy helmet of hair she smiles invitingly, with a most charming and caressing glance, as she seems to be urging us to enter the circle of her skipping-rope. She is among the supreme achievements of the mosaicist's art, and it is a pity she lies half-buried under a stairwell.

She belongs to the third century A.D., when Gaul was under Roman occupation, but the workmanship is evidently Greek, and there are traces of a Greek inscription above her head. She was found in the

village of Saint Rustice, not far from Toulouse, sometime in the last
century, but we do not know her name or where she came from
originally. She is a marine goddess, or perhaps a naiad, emerging from
the waves, wholly gentle and wholly French: and if her gown covered
her, and if there was a baby in her arms, she would appear to us like
one of those twelfth-century Virgins whose heads are inclined a little
to one side and who smile at the universe with joy and a kind of
beckoning glance.

The French genius—that peculiar mixture of strength and tenderness which we recognize as characteristically French—appears to have
flourished under the Romans in the shadow of the immense temples
and arenas, betraying nearly always a hint of Greek influence. Compare the figure of the marine goddess of Toulouse with the mausoleum
at Saint-Rémy which stands within a stone's throw of the excavated
city of Glanon. They have much the same lightness, much the same
grace. The mausoleum is not a characteristically Roman work: the
proportions have a purely Greek deftness, a way of flowering upward
into a delicate flourish. There are three registers. The bottom register
consists of reliefs, all four of them in a remarkable state of preservation. There are hunting scenes and battle scenes, crowded with figures
curiously devoid of movement, for they seem to be frozen into im-
mobility as though they were acting out some intense and passionate
charade. There is none of the violence we associate with the Perga-
mon reliefs: the sword will never fall, the spear will never leave the
fingers. In the foreground of the battle scenes there is always a naked
body of a youth, quiet in the midst of a silent battle. There is something deliberately theatrical in all these reliefs, and this has been em-
phasized by the tragic masks and cherubs reposing on the immense
wreaths hanging above the battlefield. Above these reliefs, in the
second register, is a kind of porch supported by delicately carved
Corinthian columns, and above this again is a small round temple with
twelve Corinthian columns enclosing the stone figures of two men, in
whose honor the mausoleum was erected.

There is some mystery about these men, and even today we do
not know for certain who they were. Henri Rolland, who excavated
Glanon, is inclined to believe they are Lucius and Gaius Caesar, the

grandsons of Augustus who died tragically within eighteen months of one another. Augustus hoped they would inherit the throne. He doted on them, taught them reading and swimming, sat them beside him when he took his meals, and when they went out riding it pleased the emperor to send the boys ahead, giving them precedence over himself. They were the children of his daughter Julia by Agrippa, and in their features, as we know from coins, there was the bold strength of Agrippa and the softness of Augustus curiously mingled. In the summer of A.D. 2 Lucius was sent on a mission to Spain, but got no farther than Marseilles, where he died of a fever. Gaius had been sent on a mission to the East, and in the early spring of A.D. 4 he died of fever at Limyra on the coast of Asia opposite Rhodes. Tiberius inherited the throne.

We may never know whether the mausoleum was erected for the two princes of the blood, grandsons of Augustus, but all the signs point to it. We know, for example, that in the eighteenth century, before they were restored, the two figures were of very different heights, and we know that Gaius was taller than Lucius. We know that nearby Glanon was a favorite resort of Agrippa, and the boys probably spent part of their childhood there. We find on one of the reliefs a youth holding a long staff, which may be the silver lance, *hasta argentea*, which was the badge of office of the young princes, and Henri Rolland believes that the damaged figures standing near the youth are Augustus and Julia. But all we know for certain is that the mausoleum at Saint-Rémy commemorates two youths who wielded power and fought in battles and died during the reign of Augustus Caesar; and it would not be strange if the bones of Lucius, who died in Marseilles, were not one day found within the tomb.

There is nothing funereal in the monument except on the reliefs. It has the lightness and elegance of a jewel box, and is perfectly at home with the sun and the purple hills, very tranquil. It is such a monument as might be erected to a Christian princess in Ravenna; it would not be surprising to find it near the tomb of Galla Placidia. But it stands near the ruins of a triumphal arch in a little hollow near the gates of Glanon in Provence, and of all the Roman remains in France it is the most exquisite.

Here the air is stilled, and the thundering march of the legions is forgotten. Though the monument is sixty feet high, it does not impress by its height: it impresses by its formal grace and a kind of spontaneous charm. It does not seem to be man-made, but to have grown out of the ground in a quiet place. The mystery is not so much how it came to be built as how it has survived intact for so long.

Very few of the Roman remains in France have survived intact. The heads are broken, the noses plucked away, the arenas are rubble, the grass grows between the rotting Roman stones; but the sense of vastness remains. Today the huge Roman theater at Orange looks like a quarry, little improved by the figure of Augustus, which has been placed high on the stage wall within a niche of darkness, whence he emerges with a white ghostliness to gaze down at the spectators. It is a very odd theater, with a hundred-foot wall behind the stage, and Louis XIV is supposed to have called it "the most beautiful in the kingdom," perhaps because it resembles nothing so much as a wall surrounding a prison.

The triumphal arch at Orange, the best preserved of the five triumphal arches scattered over southern France, stands on the Lyons road just outside the city. The road forks round the arch, and the trucks thunder past on both sides, shaking the poor monument to its foundations, so that little piles of crumbled stone form between the arches. There is a mystery about the arch, for no one knows for certain whether it commemorates a triumph by Julius Caesar in 49 B.C. or another by Tiberius in A.D. 21. French scholars have attempted to decipher a long-lost inscription on the northern architrave by examining the holes made for the rivets of the vanished letters, and this inscription seems to point to a victory by Tiberius over the Gallic chieftain Sacrovir, who led an army of forty thousand well-armed men, together with some slaves wearing the full armor of gladiators, against the Romans. According to Tacitus, the Roman legions simply charged the Gallic army and hacked it to pieces with axes "as though they were battering a wall." Sacrovir fled the field of battle and later killed himself in a country house near Autun, setting fire to the house before he died. On the shield of one of the Gallic warriors on the arch the name of Sacrovir can be faintly discerned. But if the arch commemorates the victory of A.D. 21, it is difficult to understand why there are so many anchors and coils of rope and prows of ships carved on it. Sacrovir was defeated on land, but seventy years before there had been a great naval battle at Marseilles, where the ships belonging to the Greek colony were rammed by a Roman fleet hastily constructed at Arles. With that battle Greek power in southern Gaul came to an end. It is more likely that the arch was erected by Julius Caesar to commemorate his victory over the Greeks, and then perhaps, in the fashion of Roman emperors, Tiberius asserted his right to the triumphal arch by writing his own inscription on it.

There is in this archway none of the delicacy to be seen in the mausoleum at Saint-Rémy. The fluted Corinthian columns seem to buckle under the weight of stone; the carved figures are harsh and angular; and the upper works squat heavily on the arches. There is neither grace nor nobility: only the surging of triumphant power. By day the flaking stone glints with a gray pallor. At night, under the floodlights, the arch comes into its own. In the floodlights it gives the impression of an ancient ship rising luminously from the depths of the sea, battered and decayed, wondrously strange, with barnacles and sea slime still clinging to it. At such times it loses the character of a triumphal monument and acquires the dignity of a shipwreck and of death.

In the very southeast corner of France, in the hills high above Monte Carlo near the Italian border, the Romans left a monument of incomparable power and grandeur. This was the trophy erected by Augustus Caesar in 6 B.C. to celebrate his conquest of all the Alpine tribes from the Adriatic to the Tyrrhenian Sea. Following a series of fiercely fought engagements in the mountains no less than forty-five tribes had fallen under his sway. For such victories no ordinary monument would serve. He ordered a vast monument crowned with a bronze image of himself. It was two hundred feet high.

Even now, though ruined beyond repair, the trophy at La Turbie (*Tropaea Augusta*) can make you catch your breath. The statue of Augustus has gone, and there are only a few vestiges of the great stepped cone on which it stood, but the huge base and some of the columns have been restored, and there is enough left to suggest the fierce grandeur of the original trophy. It can be seen for miles around, and from far out to sea, riding above Monte Carlo with a kind of brazen indifference to the lives of mere mortals crowding the coast, the white stone flashing in the sun like a great signal fire which burns on the brightest days. On moonlight nights it has a blinding glow.

For centuries men quarried the stone and built houses and fortresses from it. Stone from the trophy went to build the city of Genoa, and there are other cities in Italy even further afield which possess relics of the trophy. In the Middle Ages the Princes of Savoy transformed it into a great battlemented castle, to the annoyance of the French, who proceeded to blow it up with explosive charges in 1706, and having blown more than half of it away they left it in peace, for this quarter castle no longer presented any danger. So it remained for more than two centuries, a strange top-heavy ruin on the summit of a mountain looking out over the sea. Then an American, Dr. Edward Tuck, brought it to life again, employing the best available archeologists for the task and spending money prodigiously.

Of the original twenty-four columns only four remain, and only a handful of the letters forming the proud inscription were found, but these fitted exactly into the inscription as it was recorded by Pliny. Only one side of the great base could be reconstructed, but this was done with extraordinary care and accuracy. What has been put together is no more than the fragment of a fragment, but it rings true. There, at the end of a street, on the old Roman road which marched from the Forum in Rome to the Forum at Arles, on a high mountain, in an ancient Ligurian town, is perhaps the proudest monument conceived by a proud emperor. Sometimes, seen from a distance, it looks like a white bird with wings folded back, patiently awaiting the moment when it will soar again.

LES SAINTES MARIES

According to the legend Christianity first came to France in the little town of Les Saintes Maries at the mouth of the Rhône. One spring day, about A.D. 40, a boat without sail or oars came hurrying out of the East, bearing Mary Magdalene, Mary the mother of Saint John, and Mary Salome, the sister of the Virgin. With them came Lazarus and Martha, the venerable Bishop Maximinus, and dark-faced Sara, their servant. They were fleeing from Roman persecution, and found safety among the fishermen on this abandoned coast. They built a church, and a small town of wattle huts grew round it. In time the town came to be known as Les Saintes Maries.

We shall never know whether the three Marys really came to France. All we know for certain is that from the earliest times the Church in France claimed that their coming was a special indication of divine providence, a strange blessing, and it was firmly believed that this was the first church to be established in France. Here they had come when Christianity was still fresh with the morning dew. Here they spoke in whispers, in secret signs, speaking of a Christ they had loved and touched, his living words still ringing in their ears, before they were put down on paper. At any moment they believed he would return to them, descending from Heaven in a chariot of fire. There was a hush of expectancy, like the hush before the first dawn.

So it may have been, but in Les Saintes Maries it is the dark-faced servant girl Sara who is most vividly remembered, not by the Christians but by the gypsies who come here every year to celebrate their patroness. On that day the relics of the saints are let down on ropes from the upper chapel of the church, while the gypsies shout at the top of their lungs as they strain to touch the oaken chest; and then the chest is taken in triumph to the sea. Afterward there are processions, flamenco dances, bullfights and horse races lasting for two days. This wild, improbable fiesta has the ring of authenticity.

According to the legend Sara, Mary the mother of Saint John, and Mary Salome remained at Les Saintes Maries. Martha settled in Tarascon, where she remains to this day, while Lazarus settled in Marseilles, where all trace of him is lost, though his bones were preserved in the Cathedral at Autun. We hear of Mary Magdalene journeying to Aix in company with Bishop Maximinus, and there founding the Cathedral of Saint Sauveur. There she vanishes, only to emerge again in the high range of hills known as the Chaîne de la Sainte Baume, above Vauvenargues. In a cave in the northern face of these hills she lived out the last seventeen years of her life in prayer and meditation, comforted by the presence of a mysterious spring of cool water which sprang up the moment she knocked on the wall of the cave. At the foot of the hill Bishop Maximinus had established a small oratory; and when she died she was buried in the oratory. Not long afterward Saint Maximinus and the blind Saint Sidonius were buried beside her.

When the Saracens ravaged Provence in the eighth century, plundering and setting fire to all the towns and villages of the coast, the body of Mary Magdalene was removed from the alabaster tomb in which she had been buried and placed in the tomb of Saint Sidonius, whose body was removed elsewhere. Then the crypt itself was filled with earth. There came a time when no one any longer remembered where she was buried, though they remembered the cave in the Sainte Baume, which had become a place of pilgrimage. And when in the summer of 1254 Saint Louis passed through Provence after the Sixth Crusade, his first devotions, according to the chronicler Jean de Joinville, were paid at the Sainte Baume, in "that very high cave in the rock." This cave was the most sacred place in Provence, and it was perfectly normal that he should pause and make his devotions there.

Twenty-five years later the nephew of Saint Louis discovered the long-lost tomb of the Magdalene.

Charles d'Anjou, Prince of Salerno and Count of Provence, was a small, quiet man with a lame foot, totally unlike his father, the headstrong brother of Saint Louis. He was deeply religious and warm-hearted, the devoted father of the thirteen children of his marriage to a Hungarian princess. Her name was Maria, and it was perhaps to please her that in the turbulent summer of 1279 he set out with a small company of men from his capital at Aix to the ancient town of Saint Maximin, to see whether the Magdalene's bones lay somewhere beneath the pavement of the church. His father was fighting in Italy, and being sole regent of Provence he could do as he pleased.

On the ninth day of September he uncovered an ancient sarcophagus which bore inscriptions suggesting that here perhaps might be found the long-sought relics. Shrewdly, he did not at once open the tomb, but instead placed his seal on it and summoned a convocation of prelates, among them the famous Cardinal de Cabassoles, the friend of Petrarch, to witness the exhumation of the bones. On the eighteenth day of September the tomb was solemnly opened. Soon they found a marble sarcophagus and a small box made of cork enclosing a piece of bark on which some unknown hand had written a strange inscription:

In the year of Our Lord 716, in the month of December, very secretly in the night, when the most pious Odo was king of the French, at the time of the invasion of the perfidious nation of the Saracens, this body of the most dear and revered Mary Magdalene was translated from its own tomb of alabaster into this one of marble, out of fear of the said perfidious nation of the Saracens, because it is more secret here, the body of Sidonius having been removed.

According to contemporary historians the body was in a remarkable state of preservation. The head lay pillowed on her red-gold hair, the spot on her forehead which had been touched by Christ was still white, and green fennel was growing from her tongue. A singularly sweet smell came from her. For some reason Charles immediately ordered the body divided into three parts—the skull was placed in a golden reliquary with a crystal mask over the face, the right arm was enclosed in a reliquary of silver gilt supported by four silver-gilt lions, the rest of the body was laid in a silver casket. Told of the discovery, the King of Naples and Sicily, the father of Charles, ordered that his own jeweled crown be placed on the skull.

In the following year Charles was captured by King Peter III of Aragon and imprisoned comfortably in Barcelona for four years. His father died while he was in prison, and Sicily was lost to the kingdom, following the massacres known as the Sicilian Vespers. But when Charles regained his liberty his first thought was for the precious relics at Saint Maximin, for he believed that it was through the intercession of Mary Magdalene that he had survived the wars. He ordered the building of a cathedral over the bones.

The adventures of the bones had only just begun. Small pieces of the Magdalene found their way to all the courts of Europe, and each of the eight Popes who came to pay veneration at her shrine departed with a small keepsake. A finger was presented to Louis XI, who proclaimed her a French saint, "une fille de France." Mary Magdalene, indeed, was beginning to possess the same strange spiritual authority which later fell to Joan of Arc. It was not only that she was an undeniable protectress of the French, but the charming waywardness of her early life and her long years of penitence in the south of France seemed somehow peculiarly French; and it was remembered that she had spent more years in France than in Palestine.

Within two hundred years little of her remained in Saint Maximin. One arm found its way to the cave in the Sainte Baume; part of a lower arm went to the nuns of Nôtre Dame de Nazareth in Aix, a gift of King René. Some vertebrae went to Paris, an upper arm to Reggio, a tooth to Florence. Dismembered, she was still powerful. Saint Maximin kept the head, a few bones, a small ampoule supposed to contain some drops of blood gathered by Mary Magdalene at Golgotha. The cathedral was despoiled during the French Revolution, but a sacristan, Joseph Bastide, succeeded in hiding the sacred relics just in time. They are still there, in the same ancient Roman crypt where the lame and gentle Charles d'Anjou found them nearly seven centuries ago.

One summer day, driving out from Aix along the straight road to
Nice, I wondered whether it would be worth anyone's time to make
a detour to Saint Maximin. There was something curiously uncon-
vincing in the story of the discovery of the relics at a time when the
Pope and the King of Spain were threatening to destroy the kingdom of Provence. It was possible to have a deep respect for Charles
d'Anjou, while still wondering at his good fortune. The young
prince's careful seal on the tomb, the convenient inscription on bark,
the fennel growing from the saint's tongue—it was almost too much.
And yet, and yet, was it possible, even barely possible, that Mary
Magdalene might be lying in a small and rarely visited town in the
south of France?

I reached Saint Maximin at dusk. Darkness falls quickly on the
narrow streets of this town, which is hardly more than a village. It
was dark when I came to the cathedral, and a small rain was falling.
A sharp-featured woman in somber black was telling her beads beside one of the great Gothic pillars, and I asked her whether it was
possible to visit the crypt.

"Yes," she said, "it is possible."

She said nothing more for a while. There was only the sound of
the beads clicking in the huge empty cathedral, where only the
sacristy lamps and a few candles were shedding any light. Her face
was pale, and there were great black shadows under her eyes. At last
she seemed to awake out of her dream, and I said something about
finding the sacristan, and she said sharply: "I am in charge."

It was a bad beginning, for she looked very severe and detached,
with the pallor of someone in a state of shock. There was something
strange, too, in her movements as, a moment later, she almost ran to
the little iron gate in the north transept, which led down to the crypt.
There was a great display of jangling keys, and then we were going
down the steep flight of steps gleaming with damp, into the darkness
where one could make out an archway, the confused shapes of tombs,
flagstones worn smooth by generations of pilgrims. An electric light
clicked on. Suddenly the whole cramped crypt was bathed in a dazzling golden light, and there on a low altar fashioned out of a fourth-
century sarcophagus, supported by four gilt angels and enclosed in
a circle of gilt hair, was a brown skull glowing with specks of gold

from the swinging lamp. And most extraordinary of all, below the angels and the skull, reposed the golden mask which could be fitted over the skull, a mask of pure horror, for it had evidently been carved during the Second Empire and showed the plump, petulant, almost expressionless face of some *demi-mondaine* of the court of Napoleon III.

Gone was the jeweled crown of the King of Naples and Sicily, gone was the crystal mask of Charles d'Anjou, gone were the intricate gold reliquaries fashioned in Aix in the thirteenth century to enclose the golden arms and thighs of *la pécheresse*. All were gone, giving place to the voluptuous modeling of the worst school of sculpture of the nineteenth century.

And somehow it hardly mattered, for the brown paper-thin skull was a thing to wonder at, majestic in its gaunt dignity. Flickering there in the golden lamplight, it might have been carved by a genius to reproduce an image of Mary Magdalene. I have never seen a skull which suggested so much life. The features—for the features were recognizable—were those of a beautiful patrician, with a long face, high cheekbones, firm chin and high, wide-sweeping brows. There was no ruin in that face. If you half-closed your eyes, you saw a brown-skinned maiden of uncommon beauty gazing with a strange intensity of compassion at the passing world. In those regular features there were delicacy and sweetness, and a grave austerity; and these remained when the eyes opened wide again. The dark sockets of her eyes were not entirely lifeless. She was neither old nor young, nor of any age; belonged to no time; spoke in no intelligible tongue; had passed beyond all longing into a world where mortality no longer had any meaning; and yet in some mysterious way she belonged to the living. So sometimes in an eastern town, at dusk, one sees the hooded face of a woman leaning against the wall and gazing in a trance at the emerging stars, so lost in dreams that she seems to have left the world behind her.

This haunting face has power to move the soul. Almost it is an abstraction, like those abstractions carved by Henry Moore, the hollows and protuberances shaping into powerful planes. The quivering life in it, movement and shadow, came, I suppose, from the swinging lamp, but it was scarcely the lamp which gave authority to that face.

Haunted by the glowing face, I paid little attention to the sharp-featured woman jangling her keys and jabbering away in her toneless voice. She recited the names of the seventeen Kings and eight Popes who have knelt in adoration on the flagstones where we were standing, and much more about the crypt than I shall ever want to know. At last, abruptly, she switched off the lamp and began to climb the damp stairs leading back to the Cathedral.

Outside the rain was falling and a few neon lights were flickering. The thunder rolled far away, and faintly on the mountains of the Sainte Baume the lightning was springing. For the rest of that day, and for many days afterward, I kept wondering whether I had seen the face of Mary Magdalene, who came to France in a boat without sail or oars.

MONTSEGUR

There is a white mountain in the south of France, glittering like a pillar of snow, crowned with a white church, soaring over the emerald green meadowlands below, very sweet and beautiful. Here the skies are nearly always clear, and the air is silvery blue and tastes of wine. There is no sound except the cowbells rising clear from the meadows and valleys, and only the shadows of eagles fall on the eerie windswept summit. Bluebells grow among the rocks and yellow butterflies wander in and out of the empty doors of the church, where no services have been held for more than seven hundred years. Here and there on the snow-white walls are the traces of flames.

There is no mountain in the world like this holy mountain, which seems to wear the very face of holiness: so proud, so tender, so fierce and inaccessible, so shaped and groined it seems to be alive. For centuries holy legends crowded about the place, and many believe it was Monsalvat, the citadel of the Holy Grail; and Wagner visited it when he was writing *Parsifal*. Those who built the church called it Montségur, meaning that it was protected by God, but they also called it Tabor, the Mountain of the Transfiguration.

No one knows when the first church was built here, but the first stone of the present church was built about A.D. 1200 by the heretics who called themselves Cathari, from the Greek word meaning pure. Their heresy, if it was a heresy, had developed over the centuries and

Goddess of Vienne

Mausoleum at Saint-Rémy

Monument of Augustus, La Turbie

Arch of Triumph, Orange

Moissac

Jeremiah—from the
Moissac doorway
central pillar

Christ in Majesty (above)
and The Blessed—details from the architrave

The Great Vase of Vix

contained many traces of the Gnosticism which abounded in the eastern Mediterranean at the time of Christ. They were Christians, and read the Scriptures literally, believing, as the early Christians believed, that the Second Coming was at hand and therefore the life of the spirit was of infinitely greater value than the earthly life, and nothing was to be gained by loving the flesh. They rejected the ornaments of religion: their rituals were of astonishing simplicity. They rejected the Mass, the Virgin Birth, Baptism, Absolution and Purgatory. They even rejected the sacrament of marriage. They believed in penance, the life of the spirit, a perfect dedication to Christ. They renounced property, and by renouncing temporal power they rendered themselves very nearly helpless in the face of their enemies, though having no fear of death, and even welcoming it, they were prepared to fight for their beliefs.

The faith of the Cathari was not an isolated phenomenon. All over Europe, at all times, there have been sects determined to cut through theological complexities and to live lives of perfect dedication. They saw the world clearly, in black and white. The world was evil: into this world had come the pure Word of Christ, who was very God, and therefore it was inconceivable that He suffered on the Cross or was resurrected in the flesh. Christ was God's ghostly presence, a phantom, almost pure spirit, to be worshiped and imitated but never adored with intricate and costly ceremonies. Their priests wore no vestments, and there were no sacraments, nor candles, nor incense. When the worshipers met together the eldest present broke the bread and gave it to the assembled men and women with the words: "Thanks be to the God of our Jesus Christ. May the spirit be with us all." They practiced penances for their sins, but they were simple penances. "Penance, true, chaste and virginal, is alone capable of bringing forth Sons of God," wrote one of the Cathari. They read the Gospels, especially the Gospel of John, but they also possessed their own books, including *The Book of the Two Principles*, which were the principles of good and evil, and *The Secret Supper*, which consists of a brief colloquy between John and Christ and includes passages of quite extraordinary poetic feeling. "The sun is the Prince of this world and his throne, and the moon is the law of Moses, and the stars are the spirits who minister unto the Prince. There will be no place for the Apostles to reign, but Christ, the Son of God, is the seven-fold Sun, and He shall reign." So they wrote in those extraordinary books which mingle a fervent simplicity with Gnosticism, Manichaeanism, and the exalted visions of The Revelation of Saint John.

Inevitably a form of priesthood evolved. Those who were more dedicated than others formed an inner circle and were called the "perfect." They received the *consolamentum*, the laying on of hands, and they promised to dedicate themselves to God and the Holy Scriptures, never to lie or swear or touch a woman, never to kill an animal, never to eat meat or eggs (since they are the products of the act of reproduction), but only vegetables and fish, and they were to sleep fully clothed on the ground. There followed the *endura*, a fast of forty days, to prepare them for a life lived wholly in the spirit and to bring them closer to God. When the "perfect" felt death approaching, they fasted not so much to die more quickly but in order to be in a state of grace when death occurred.

By 1200 Catharism was a force to be reckoned with. All northern Italy and southern France were honeycombed with the sect. The common people, weary of the ornate ceremonies of the Church, were intoxicated with the simple faith of the Cathari. Their spiritual needs were answered by the "perfect," who wandered in their black robes from one small community to another in search of converts. They were men formidably learned in simple things, careless of danger, cunning in their denunciations of the Church, and extraordinarily gentle in their behavior; and their faces reflected the enviable purity of their souls. Great nobles like Count Raymond of Toulouse and Count Raymond-Roger of Foix gave their protection to the sect, and almost the entire aristocracy of southern France was devoted to the heresy. The Church was in danger. "These heretics are worse than the Saracens!" exclaimed Pope Innocent III. On March 10, 1208, he proclaimed a crusade with the object of putting to death all those, numbering perhaps half a million, who belonged to the sect and refused to abjure the heresy.

By July, 1209, a vast army of Crusaders had gathered at Montpellier with orders to burn every city from the Mediterranean to the

Pyrenees which harbored the Cathari. The leader of the army was Simon de Montfort, a young French nobleman who by his marriage to an English heiress also bore the title of Earl of Leicester. The first stop was Béziers, where they demanded that the city fathers hand over the 222 Cathari known to be in the city. The city fathers refused, and Simon de Montfort gave orders for the massacre of every man, woman and child of the city's 20,000 inhabitants. Not even the priests were spared. When Abbé Arnaud-Amalric, the head of the Cistercian monastic order, was asked how to distinguish the heretics from the faithful, he answered: "Kill them all! God will recognize his own!" Then it was the turn of Carcassonne, which fared better, for the inhabitants had time to flee. Then all the villages and castles in the neighborhood were taken, and the conquered territory came into the possession of Simon de Montfort. Catharism flourished. It flourished all the more because the Church was pitiless.

For thirty-five terrible years the Crusaders brought fire and sword to the south of France. Heretics, when captured, were burned at the stake: they died quietly and eagerly. Catharism survived Simon de Montfort, who was killed in Toulouse by a woman who threw a stone at him from the city walls: it must have been a very large stone, for the chronicler reports that it crushed his helmet and broke his head, and "he fell down of a sudden and instantly turned black." But Simon was followed by his equally vengeful son Amaury, and the King of France joined the crusade, eager to acquire the rich territories in the south, and soon the vast military power of the Pope and the King of France began to take effect. Altogether five crusades were sent against the Cathari, who were hunted down like wild animals. They took to the woods, the forests and the hills. They hid in the valleys of the Pyrenees and in the crevices of the mountains, and no place was safe except the white church on Montségur.

The church was safe because all the approaches could be easily defended. On one side there was a sheer drop of four hundred feet, on the other side were narrow valleys where a handful of men could hold up advancing armies. The holy mountain became their refuge, the source of their supplies, a hiding place for their treasure and their holy books. Here men came when they believed they were dying, or when their communities were destroyed. It was the headquarters of the saintly Guilhabert de Castres, who kept the flames of Catharism alive. He was a very old man, but he possessed remarkable powers of endurance and could march the whole night to reach some wretched villagers whose faith was trembling in the balance, and he had great influence among the nobility. When Count Raymond of Toulouse was ordered to destroy Montségur, he sent only a small, ill-equipped token army. His sympathies lay with the Cathari however much he protested his allegiance to the Pope.

By 1242 the Pope and the King of France had lost all patience. The "most unholy and most damnable heresy" of Catharism was still gaining converts. The young, half-English Count Raymond of Toulouse had been forced to submit to the Church, being led down the aisle of Nôtre Dame "naked except for his shift" to beg absolution for the sin of having sustained the heretics. As further punishment he was given ten thousand troops and ordered to take Montségur by storm. Ironically, the man who had given most aid to the heretics was forced to become their executioner.

The siege of Montségur lasted ten months. There were never more than three hundred armed men in the church, and never less than ten thousand in the tents below. The army arrived during the first days of May, 1243. At first they hoped to starve the defenders into surrender. They would wait until the food gave out and the summer suns dried up the wells. There were sporadic attacks which were beaten back, and by the end of the long summer none of the attackers had come within hailing distance of the church. All through the summer and autumn the defenders were constantly receiving supplies from men who passed secretly through the lines. They came at night along footpaths unknown to the enemy or climbed the cliffs with the aid of ropes let down from the church.

Within the church transformed into a fortress the daily life went on as usual. Guilhabert de Castres had died, and his place was taken by Bertran d'en Marti, who presided over the Cathar ceremonies and continued to bring new converts into the fold. Among the converts was one of the daughters of Raymond de Perella, lord of Montségur. Her name was Esclarmonde, and she had been ill from birth.

Her mother, Corba de Perella, and her grandmother, the Marquesia de Lantar, also became Cathari, and so did Philippa, the wife of Pierre-Roger de Mirepoix, who was in command of the armed men inside the church. Most of these soldiers and sergeants-at-arms were sympathizers, not believers. They fought because they had seen too many of their friends burned at the stake.

In November the tide began to turn, for in that month some mercenaries from the Basque country were able to capture a shoulder of the mountain only five hundred feet from the walls of the church, and here Durand, Bishop of Albi, a man with a great experience of military strategy, was able to install a stone-throwing machine. But this advantage was offset by the arrival of new troops led by the engineer Bertran de la Beccalaria, who set up stone-throwing machines inside the church. He had forced his way through the lines. Then late in December the Basques succeeded in climbing the sheer cliffs on a moonless night and took the church tower by surprise, massacring everyone in it. Jean Bernat, a traitor, had shown them the way up the precipitous cliffs.

The Basques remained in the tower, but the fighting went on. The Bishop of Albi brought up more stone throwers, which tore great holes in the roof, but had little effect on the rugged walls. A few more soldiers came to help the defenders, but the end was not far off. All through February, day and night, the fire arrows were falling into the church and boulders were crashing against the walls. "The dragon's head, Montségur, must be cut off," Blanche de Castille had decreed, and the time for the blood letting had come.

On March 1, 1244, Pierre-Roger de Mirepoix went out under a flag of truce to make the best terms he could. They were unusual terms, for the lives of all the soldiers were spared, and so too were the lives of all those who abjured the heresy. The fortress-church was to become the possession of the Pope and the King of France. Finally, permission was granted to the defenders to remain on Montségur for a further two weeks. It was hoped that the Cathari would, in those two weeks of respite, see the error of their ways.

They did not see the error of their ways. As the days passed, more and more of the defenders embraced Catharism, receiving the *con-*

solamentum from the hands of Bertran d'en Marti, who moved among them like a spirit sent from God. It was remarked that the defenders were strangely quiet during those last days. Those who were to die calmly distributed their possessions among those who would remain alive. They were small gifts, and we hear of Bertran d'en Marti giving his supplies of oil, salt, pepper and wax to Pierre-Roger de Mirepoix. On the night of March 15 Pierre Authier, treasurer of the Cathari, was lowered down the cliff walls by rope with three other men under orders to make their way to the Château d'Ussat in the High Pyrenees, where several of the faithful had already taken refuge. He was to guard the treasure carefully and wait there until the time when the Cathari would one day return to the valleys. A beacon light on the peak of Mont Barthélemy would signify that they had arrived safely in territory where the King's men would never follow them.

Just before dawn they saw the beacon light burning on the mountain top, and this signal of their deliverance was also the signal for the largest *auto-da-fé* known up to this time, for on the sloping meadows at the foot of the mountain a vast field of fagots had been laid. Two hundred and sixteen of the "perfect" came down the mountain and quietly laid themselves down on the stake, and in case any of them should think of escaping at the last moment ropes were tied round their wrists and ankles. The procession was led by Bertran d'en Marti, and not far from the head of the procession walked Corba de Perella, her mother the Marquesia de Lantar, and her sick daughter Esclarmonde, whose name means "to bring light to the world." Then the field of fagots was set alight, and the soldiers withdrew to a safe distance while the flames leaped and a great cloud of smoke hid the church from sight. It does not take long to burn two hundred people. By noon there was only a smoldering white field of wood ash on the slope of a white mountain.

The holy citadel of the Cathari had been destroyed, but Catharism survived. For another half century the Inquisitors were fully occupied, perpetually discovering new nests of Cathari and destroying them. The Cathari refused to bow to pressure; they could only be exterminated: and many who fled France returned secretly. Some crossed the Pyrenees and went over into Spain, others made their way over the Alps to Lombardy, and a few went to Germany and England, where they were known as Bonhommes. They never wholly perished, and in the fullness of time they provided the seed which burst forth in the Reformation.

I came to Montségur one day in late autumn when the sky was high and of that pure silvery blue which comes from the reflected snows of the Pyrenees. There was no traffic along the winding road from Lavelanet, which for mile upon mile is bordered with thick pine forests. I was in no special mood of expectation, for over the years I had read a great deal about the mountain and seen perhaps twenty photographs. What I did not know, and could not have guessed, was the extraordinary beauty of the mountain.

The first glimpse of it was even a little frightening, for I had not expected to see that white face set on broad shoulders peering through the pine trees at a turning of the road. Then, as we followed the road, the mountain seemed to be turning its several faces to the sun. One moment it was sharp and pointed, the next it was gracefully curved, and then again it grew heavy and rugged, more like a white muscular shoulder. It changed with every aspect, becoming even more beautiful as we approached. It was like a sculpture of a human head which can be turned around and remains wonderfully vivid from whatever angle it is seen.

The mountain exceeded all expectation; so too did the ruined church, whose white walls flashed in the sun and seemed to melt in the silver of the heavens. Indeed, from below, the church does not look ruined. It sits squarely across two humps on the mountain top, the calcareous stone as white as on the day it was completed. Sitting there low to the ground, possessing a monumental grandeur, it might be taken for a fine example of modern architecture.

All the top of the mountain is a blaze of white ribbed stone, but today there are green fields marching up the slope, where the sheep graze. Not far from the motor road, just before the steep rise, is the

Pré de Crémats, "the meadow of the burning," where a small altar of stones gathered from within the church has been erected. On the altar someone has carved words written in the ancient French spoken by the Cathari:

ALS CATARS

ALS MARTIRS

DEL PUR AMOR

CRESTIAN

16 MARS 1244

Below this inscription to "the martyrs of the pure love of Christ" the same hand has carved the badge of the Cathari, a five-pointed star above three crosses, an eye, and a hand holding the Gospels. Someone long ago had laid a wreath on the altar, but now it was dry and yellow, flaking into powder.

There is a steep climb to the top of the mountain along a stone footpath: the stones are loose and the path skirts the edge of the cliff. That day the sun was blinding, its light scattering off the stones. There was no sound except the clear notes of distant sheep bells. An eagle flew overhead in slow, sweeping circles, and when its shadow fell on the blinding stones it seemed to obliterate them. It was then, seeing the eagle, that I remembered the mysterious chill which comes to all travelers in Delphi, another mountain where the eagles soar over gleaming chasms. There, too, one has the sense of the earth falling away, of being poised on the topmost crown of the earth, and of entering a silent kingdom where all the normal laws of existence are held in abeyance. There are mountains which by their very shape and by a strange configuration of the land around them have the power to purify.

But I was not thinking of purification as I climbed those steep, crumbling steps which led to the top of the mountain, nor even of the extraordinary grandeur of the place, which seemed but a stone's throw from the Pyrenees already white with the first heavy snowfalls. There was the great church sitting astride the whole top of the mountain, and it did not look spoiled. The walls were solid. There was not a stone out of place in the small arched doorway. The façade was clean, powerful, untouched, magnificent in its solidity and strength. More than seven hundred years have passed, and it looked as though it had been built yesterday.

And inside it was the same, clean and white except where grass and small trees were growing. There was no roof, of course, but the roof had collapsed long before the day when the two hundred Cathari walked down to "the meadow of the burning." You could still climb the two solid stairways leading up to the top of the walls, which were five feet wide in places. Basque mercenaries had occupied the tower while the Cathari still lived in the rest of the church, and I wondered how they could have remained there for three months until I saw the thickness of the tower walls, and even today there is no way of reaching the tower except from outside. Below the tower is the cliff which the Basques climbed on a moonless winter night, shivering with fright the next morning when they looked down and saw the perilous road they had traveled.

Chroniclers of the time speak of underground caverns and tunnels honeycombing the mountain from secret doors in the church floor, but no one has ever discovered them. Montségur would be worth excavating, for there is no doubt that Cathari relics lie underground. As for the treasure which Pierre Authier carried away on the night before the surrender, no trace of it was ever found, and no one can guess what kind of treasure it was, though it was more likely to have been sacred books than golden chalices. The church remains, and the two books of the Cathari scriptures, and that is all. They wrote no histories, and what little we know about them has been compiled from the documents of the Inquisitors, who were their enemies. And somehow it seems perfectly appropriate that we should know them best through the great church they built on the holy mountain.

Yellow butterflies swarmed over the empty church and the blue eagle soared in great, mindless circles, and it was very quiet on the mountain top. One had the impression of being on a ship which, after long voyaging, had come at last to quiet waters, and indeed the long, narrow church without transepts and with a raised forecastle looked very much like a ship secure in its anchorage. The winter winds pound the stone walls, the snowdrifts cover them, and you would think the frosts would split them, but neither time nor nature has affected them. A thousand years from now Montségur will still be standing there, unchanged.

I climbed down the mountain and went to call on the mayor of the little red-roofed village at its feet. He was a well-set man, stocky and red-cheeked. He was a peasant from the region, and he had a way of walking through the village like a grand seigneur showing off his property. It was a poor village, but he was proud of it. The villagers treated him like a friend.

"It's strange," he said. "When I was a boy, no one ever came here. Now every summer they come from Toulouse and Paris and from foreign countries, and sometimes they go off to the peak of Mont Barthélemy and start digging. They never find anything. I am sure of that, because our peasants have been digging for centuries, and not one of them ever found anything. We have our ways of knowing about these things."

I asked whether anyone had been excavating in the church recently, and he laughed softly.

"They've been digging there for centuries," he said, "and they never found anything, not even bones. It's strange how they came and left nothing behind. People have even dug up the *Pré de Crémats* in the hope of finding the ashes of the martyrs who were burned there, but they never found the ashes. It's true. There's no trace of them anywhere, and sometimes I wonder whether they really lived up there on the mountain."

An old bright-eyed man was leading a goat to the village slaughter-house. The old man had a fine wrinkled face the color of ripe apples.

"How old do you think the man is?" the mayor asked.

"Seventy."

"No, he's eighty-five. You ought to come here and stay all the year round. *No one ever dies here.*"

In the shadow of Montségur anything could happen, but I was a little startled.

"It's true. We're all peasants, and we work on the slopes of the mountains, and that's good for the health, and the air is pure here. Go to the cemetery, and you'll see we all die at a very great age. In

Paris people die young, but here they never die before ninety. So they are going to build a sanatorium, a big one, maybe on the slopes of Montségur, and if you come back in five years you won't see a poverty-stricken village any more, because we will all be working in the sanatorium."

He showed me his correspondence with Paris in the little cluttered office which served as the village *mairie*—long letters full of statistics on wind, sunlight, atmospheric pressure and air pollution, but I am not sure the sanatorium will ever be built, or even whether it is desirable. It may be better to leave the mountain untouched, as a memorial to a brilliant people and a way of life which has vanished forever.

MOISSAC

There was a time, not so long ago, when no one bothered very much about the Romanesque churches of France. The lover of medieval architecture went to Coutances, Rheims, Sens, Chartres and the Sainte Chapelle, admiring the delicacy and height of the pillars, the glow of the windows, the sustained imaginative effort which produced those white and soaring emblems of man's hope. We are not so hopeful now, and sometimes these Gothic churches seem only too successful in proving the skill of medieval architects in raising pillars to impossible heights. Romanesque churches are more humble, heavier, earthier. They have put away soaring pride and are more concerned with the practical matter of the salvation of souls in a world given over to evil. While Gothic is a young man stretching up adoring arms to heaven, Romanesque is an old man bent in prayer. Gothic is carefree, Romanesque full of cares. And while Gothic points to heaven, Romanesque seems to point with unerring aim to the mysteries and tribulations of the human heart.

So it is no wonder that all over France there is a resurgence of interest in Romanesque churches, which are often far from the big cities. Today students on bicycles collect Romanesque churches as in another day they would collect stamps. I know a retired French admiral who thinks no day well spent unless he is studying them, or wandering from one to another, or drawing up plans of their walls, or trying to trace the journeys of the obscure and nameless sculptors whose work can be recognized in churches far away from one another. He will talk of the Sainte Chapelle as though it were nothing more than a jewel box and of Chartres as a mathematical monstrosity. He has commanded the most modern ships in battle, and he would give a small fortune to talk to those forgotten sculptors and architects and solve some of the mysteries of Romanesque art.

There are mysteries everywhere in Gothic architecture: we do not know why quite suddenly the walls were opened out to receive the sunlight or how the architects went about solving the complex problems involving stresses. But the mysteries of Romanesque belong to another order altogether, for we can trace its origins through the Roman basilicas and we can watch its development step by step. What we do not know, and can scarcely guess at, is how these architects and sculptors were able to speak with so much authority. They spoke as men speak when their faith is absolute. They saw with complete certainty things we can only guess at.

The truly great works of religious art are exceedingly rare. One can marvel at the God who floats in the clouds above the Sistine Chapel pointing a finger at Adam, who awakens from sleep with all the languor of a young Renaissance prince, but if we set this portrait of God against the great stone-carved Trimurti in the cave at Elephanta, we are compelled to recognize a greater power, a greater sense of God's absolute divinity, in the work of the Indian sculptor. There are no easy ways to express the power and the majesty of God. The God whose power extends over the entire universe, the absolute and eternal Father of Lights, the creator of all things, the hand which moves upon the heavens and writes the names of the furthermost stars—this God is so much beyond the scope of our imaginations that we would be prepared to believe it was beyond the scope of the very greatest artist. Yet here and there, at different periods in the world's history, this God has been depicted, usually by artists whose names remain unknown. I think of the Trimurti at Elephanta, and the great mosaic of the Pantocrator in the dome of the Church of the Golden Laurels at Daphni near Athens, and of the unearthly beauty and authority in the blue-robed *bod-*

dhisattvas found in the caves at Tunhuang by Sir Aurel Stein which are now in the British Museum—these were the only perfect expressions of divine majesty I knew until I came to Moissac, a small town in southwestern France. There, over the western gate of St. Peter's church, there exists a representation of God in majesty which must rank with the very greatest works of religious art ever produced.

This royal gate was fashioned by an unknown artist about A.D. 1120, taking as his text a stupendous passage from The Revelation of St. John:

Behold, a throne was set in heaven, and one sat on the throne. And he that sat was to look upon like a jasper and a sardine stone: and there was a rainbow round about the throne, in sight like unto an emerald. And round about the throne were four and twenty seats: and upon the seats I saw four and twenty elders sitting, clothed in white raiment; and they had on their heads crowns of gold. And out of the throne proceeded lightnings and thunderings and voices: and there were seven lamps of fire burning before the throne, which are the seven Spirits of God. And before the throne there was a sea of glass like unto crystal: and in the midst of the throne, and round about the throne, were four beasts, full of eyes before and behind. And the first beast was like a lion, and the second beast like a calf, and the third beast had a face as a man, and the fourth beast was like a flying eagle. And the four beasts had each of them six wings about him; and they were full of eyes within: and they rest not day and night, saying, Holy, holy, holy, Lord God Almighty, which was, and is, and is to come. And when those beasts give glory and honour and thanks to him that sat on the throne, who liveth for ever and ever, the four and twenty elders fall down before him that sat on the throne, and worship him that liveth for ever and ever, and cast their crowns before the throne, saying, Thou art worthy, O Lord, to receive glory and honour and power: for thou hast created all things, and for thy pleasure they are and were created.

One would have thought it beyond any sculptor's power to depict the moment of the Second Coming, the sudden blaze of glory with Christ enthroned in His ultimate majesty, as an event moving from time into eternity. One would have thought it impossible to convey a world so final, so rapt in adoration, so eloquent of human aspirations, so breathtakingly simple. Time has come to an end, and the

God of wrath and terror and pity sits in judgment over the blessed and the damned, one hand holding the book of the law and the other raised in blessing, and it is beyond belief that we are in the presence of the Second Coming, but it is so. This Christ is absolute Christ. He has come only a moment ago, for the folds of His gown have not yet settled; and He wields no scepter, and possesses no instruments of power, and gazes neither to the left nor right, and is content at the world's end. There is an expression on His face of extraordinary wide-eyed calm, and of power so resolute that He has only to raise His left hand and millions of worlds would come into existence. But the hand lies heavy on the book, and there will be no more worlds, for time has come to an end.

The unknown sculptor has used extraordinary means to depict an extraordinary scene. While Christ and the two towering angels beside him remain calm, everything else is in violent movement. Stone is converted into sheets of flame, and this flamelike effect is achieved by fierce, rippling lines which move continuously across the gateway, echoing and reflecting one another, flinging themselves at last upon the person of Christ from all directions. The four and twenty elders are represented in three registers, but these registers have been so contrived that even though the elders are sitting down and calmly adoring Christ, they give an impression of leaping tongues of flame: and so it is too with the evangelists, the lion, the eagle, the calf and "the beast with the face of a man," who are all turning abruptly and fiercely to adore Christ, and the very turning and twisting of their bodies gives life to the carving—life of an extreme, dangerous and hallucinatory kind. The eagle is anatomically impossible, but how powerfully he turns his neck to gaze upon the face of Christ, and with what vigor he thrusts his whole body into a kind of backward leap, ready to climb upon Christ's shoulders to proclaim, however uselessly—for Christ has already proclaimed it— that the end of the world has come and the reign of God has become manifest at last. "The beast with the face of a man" is wholly human, but he too is flung back upon himself as he performs an intricate and improbable dance, one arm suspended in mid-air, one knee pointed toward the vanished world, while his head is thrown back in a violent gesture of adoration. Remove the Gospel makers from the scene—the heraldic and legendary lion, eagle, calf and man, all twisted and coiled in impossible positions—and the legendary life will have gone from it. In their violence and in the calm of Christ below the thundering heavens lies the complete statement of the artist's vision, and the attendant elders, and all the other powerful carvings which go to make up this gateway, are no more than flames lighting the greater fire.

But while the mind and the eye are immediately attracted to the powerful and commanding image of Christ attended by the turbulent and triumphant evangelists, it is the orderly composition of the whole gateway which finally commands our admiration. It is a symphony in honor of the Second Coming in many movements, with many contrasting themes, composed by a single composer of prodigious brilliance, who was not afraid to employ deliberate dissonances and sudden violent alterations of mood, selecting elements from widely different cultures and fusing them into a whole by the pressure of his powerful imagination. The face of Christ with the stiffly curling beard derives across the centuries from the portraits of ancient Persian and Sumerian kings; the delicate scroll patterns were first designed by Sasanian silversmiths; those elongated angels can be seen on Byzantine ivories; and the squat kings could have been the work of Gallo-Roman artists twelve hundred years before the gateway at Moissac was erected. But it is not important that there are derivative elements. What is important is the single flame which shines on all of them.

Only an artist of prodigious daring would have placed below the tympanum a heavy marble lintel with eight immense rosettes carved upon it. These rosettes have a classical beauty, and you might imagine they have been borrowed from some long-abandoned Roman temple until you observe that strange dragons have taken up their positions at either end, and they are in fact blowing these fantastically intricate rosettes out of their mouths. The rosettes therefore represent worlds and universes which have come to birth and which are now passing away into the fires of the Last Judgment, as thistledown vanishes into the summer air. Local botanists maintain that these rosettes are modeled on a variety of thistles growing in the mountains nearby, which the country folk call *charlemagnes*, giving them even now the name of a beloved sovereign; in ancient days these thistles were believed to be a sovereign remedy against plague.

Ordinarily the lintel would have been supported on columns, but the artist, very conscious of the need to continue that jagged, spiraling, flamelike line to the ground, has invented entirely new kinds of columns. The side columns are overwhelmingly and almost insolently plain, cusped in the Moorish fashion and decorated with miniature portraits of Saint Peter and Isaiah, both in the familiar postures of withdrawal and adoration with their heads bent toward the towering Christ above them. The central pillar is an extraordinarily intricate design of six crossed lions and lionesses against a background of thistles. The lions have their mouths wide open, ready to bite anyone who enters the church. They are not there for decorative effect alone. They are there to remind the faithful of the imminence of death. *"Libera eas de ore leonis,"* says the offertory of the Mass for the Dead. "Deliver them from the lion's mouth, that hell swallow them not up, that they fall not into darkness. . . ." Those lions and lionesses seem gentle enough until you view them from the sides and see the stretched muscles of their necks and the hideous hunger of their open mouths. On the sides Saint Paul and Jeremiah are depicted, and it is worth while to pause over the figure of Jeremiah, for it is one of the great masterpieces of French sculpture.

Everything about him is flowing: the beard, the hair, the scroll, the draperies. His feet are crossed and his head is bent, and he seems to be dancing like David before the Ark. This is not the Jeremiah of the thundering imprecations or the dreadful visions; it is the other, quieter Jeremiah who turns appealingly to God and says: "I know that the way of man is not in himself: it is not in man that walketh to direct his steps." So long-legged Jeremiah dances his holy dance, rapt in adoration, following in the footsteps of the Lord, and unmindful of the lions roaring at his side. He is an oriental prophet, but he is wholly the product of a characteristically French imagination, combining power with elegance. Though invisible from outside, he belongs to the grand design of the gateway by virtue of his prophecies.

There was a time when this immense gateway gleamed with a

profusion of colors, for the Romanesque sculptors, like the ancient
Greeks, thought stone naked unless it was painted. We know what
the colors were, though not a trace of paint remains, for they are
clearly indicated in The Revelation of Saint John. Christ must have
been in gold, with rainbow colors round the throne, the squat kings
wore white vestments with golden crowns and their faces were
purple red like the goblets they hold in their hands, and the feet of
Christ reposed on a silvery sea. The entire surface of the gateway
was garishly painted with such a shimmering of gold and purple and
emerald green and silver that the effect must have been blinding, and
the worshiper entering the church may have been too dazzled by the
Second Coming to pray for his own salvation. Today the gateway is
lit at night by powerful lamps directed from a building opposite,
and something of the original splendor is recreated by electricity.
Today the figures glimmer with dusky gold where previously they
shone with pure gold and the richest colors on the palette.

The rare visitors who come to Moissac are not content to see only
the gateway. There are innumerable Romanesque carvings, and there
are even Carolingian mosaics near the altar. There is a staggering
richness of design in all the carvings, though it must be admitted that
the unknown sculptor of the royal gateway is no longer present in
the minor works; nor is he present in the cloister behind the church,
the largest and most perfect in all of France. I had thought the
cloister at Saint Trophime in Arles was the loveliest, but it has not
the spaciousness of Moissac, nor have the carved capitals the same
quiet richness and clarity. Ansquitil, Abbot of Moissac, built his
cloister about A.D. 1100, some eighty years before the cloister at
Saint Trophime came into existence, a quarter of a century before
the royal gateway was completed. No portrait of him has survived,
though there are portraits of his successor and predecessor, but the
cloister portrays him well enough: he was a man who liked a certain
quiet majesty, and he enjoyed wide spaces to walk in when meditat-
ing, and he loved water, for he built a great fountain in his cloister
which survived until the seventeenth century. He died in A.D. 1115
and therefore never saw the great tympanum which was planned
during his abbacy.

But it is that gateway which one remembers most, and sometimes I think that if everything in France had to be destroyed and only one object was allowed to remain, I would choose that gateway. There, if anywhere, is to be found the sense of authentic majesty and splendor. And if only two things were allowed to remain, I would choose the Sainte Chapelle as well, and if there were three things I would include the Blue Virgin of Chartres. In those three things, a chapel, a gate and a window, all that is most magnificent in France seems to be concentrated.

I came to Moissac one afternoon when the clouds were low and a storm was brewing, in a car driven by a man who resembled a defrocked medieval priest. He had a small craggy, monumental face such as might have been carved by a Romanesque sculptor. He had no faith in traffic regulations and raced along the winding road from Montauban with implicit faith that all the other vehicles on the road would get out of the way; and so they did, but only because I was praying. He was more than half mad and very kind, and like all Frenchmen he liked to talk about his native city.

I had spent the morning in Montauban, and it pleased him to examine me on what I had seen in that hilly city. Had I seen the Jardin des Plantes? Had I entered the church which is ornamented with an immense painting by Ingres? I had seen none of these things and he frowned disapprovingly, but relented a little when I said I had seen the sculptures of Bourdelle and the other paintings by Ingres in the local museum. The Bourdelle statues were among his best, and if one likes Ingres there are more than enough of his paintings, drawings and water colors to keep one busy for many days and even for many months, since the artist left all his personal effects and his entire collection of five thousand drawings to the museum. Among these personal effects was a small heap of gray ashes which he had gathered from the tomb of the painter Raphael: they lie on a mirror in a gold frame and look like curiously colored flakes of straw. There, too, standing in a glass case, was the famous *violin d'Ingres* which he played when he was weary of painting, and far too many laurel crowns of hammered gold.

But it was not about Montauban or Ingres that I wanted him to speak. I asked him about Moissac, and he replied that he had visited it only once in his life to take some foreigners to see the great gateway. They were Finns, and they had journeyed all the way from Helsingfors to study the gate and take photographs and stand in studious admiration before those ancient carvings. "They were six or seven tow-headed Finns jabbering away like mad, and sometimes they would yell and point out something and they would get together and make drawings and take more photographs. *Monsieur*, why should the Finns be so excited about a little lost village in southwestern France?"

Though it was still early in the afternoon the light was fading when we reached Moissac, for the clouds were heavy. The great gateway could only barely be seen, for most of the carving lies under a heavy overhanging arch. The chauffeur knew what to do. He drove the car close to the gate and directed his powerful car lamps on the carvings, making them glow in a strange golden milky light. Later, when it was growing dark, the more powerful lights from a building opposite were turned on, but it was the first impression, produced by the car lamps, which was electrifying, and which remains in my memory. For a few moments, until the light settled, the whole gateway seemed to be sheeted in brilliant gold.

Later in the evening it rained, and I took refuge in a small museum near the church which can be reached along a stone-flagged pathway through a wild garden. There was nothing of very great interest in the museum, nor could there be, since the church had survived largely intact, and the whole church was a treasure chest containing so many treasures within its own walls that nothing of value was left over. The guardian of the museum was a small, bustling, exceedingly pleasant woman who let me loose to stumble over the creaking floorboards and the rickety stairs, and examine the local peasant costumes gathering dust in the glass cases. It was a relief to be out of the rain. It was a relief, too, not to be looking at the gateway or the cloisters, for they are works of such consummate art that it is best to come to them again and again, to avoid being exhausted by their beauty.

When I came down the stairs, there was a girl standing in the doorway. She looked about eighteen, and she wore a white belted raincoat. The lightning was flickering behind her, and gusts of wind and rain were blowing through the open door. The girl stood there smiling, her face gleaming with rain, and in that light, in these strange surroundings, she gave an impression of overwhelming beauty. I was about to pass her and go out into the night when she said, speaking very rapidly and with a slight lisp: "What on earth were you doing upstairs?" I explained as well as I could, and she burst out laughing. It was a very pleasant laugh, and I began to think there were advantages in staying a little longer in this odd, creaking museum.

"I saw the lights coming on, so I hurried over," she said. "We don't often open the museum at night, do we?" she went on, addressing the bustling woman who had led me into the house. "We don't have many visitors in Moissac, and at night, too!" She had high cheekbones, a rounded forehead, and a delicately carved chin, and it occurred to me that she looked like some of the early portraits of Joan of Arc. The rain was still dripping down her face. She seemed to be trembling with some secret amusement as she asked me what I had seen in Moissac and what impression it had made on me, and where I was going, and fifty other questions all spoken in a low rapid musical voice which had something of the effect of a supercharged machine gun. I have never heard anyone speak French so rapidly.

Soon she was delivering a lecture about the gateway, with more expert knowledge than one would expect from an eighteen-year-old girl. At one point I was bold enough to interrupt her, quoting from a book about Moissac I had found in New York. It is an admirable book, and I had fallen under the spell of the text and the illustrations.[1]

"Well, that's what I wrote three years ago, but I've learned a great deal since then," she said. "I wrote the book. I'm the curator of Moissac. You see, I had to write the book very quickly."

She went on, as rapidly as ever, to talk about the design of the gateway and how it must have appeared when it was built. She was convinced that two artists had been at work, the central figure of Christ and the angels being by one sculptor, and the rest by another. She had even found the presumed portraits of the sculptors in two

---

[1] *Quercy Roman*, par Marguerite Vidal. La Nuit des Temps, 1959.

small figures hidden away in the massive decoration, each holding his sculptor's mallet, and by some curious quirk of the medieval masonic guilds each had one foot shod and the other bare. And as she talked, and the rain thudded outside, it became perfectly clear that she was in love with the great doorway and she would be perfectly content to study it for the rest of her life. She loved it with a quiet and determined passion, determined to make it yield its secrets. There was still so much to be discovered, so many problems to be solved. There was Persian influence on the sculptures. There was a church in Catalonia with a tympanum which seemed to have been carved by the same sculptors. Here and there, at Autun and Vézelay, and in scattered churches all over southern France, there were clues which would have to be followed up. How did Persian influence enter France? Why was Jeremiah dancing? To what school belonged these unnamed and mysterious sculptors?

"But the worst problem of all is the conservation of the gateway," she said. "Already it is flaking away, and there is so little we can do. There are chemicals in the air which eat the stone away, and this is something quite new, and we are ill prepared to cope with it. Just think, in a hundred years' time it may have perished!"

I left an hour later. She stood in the doorway, still wearing a glistening raincoat and smiling her enchanted smile, the youngest and most beautiful curator I have ever seen. And while the half-mad medieval priest drove through the night, roaring at sixty miles an hour along the narrow roads deep in water and throwing up great silvery bow waves, I reflected that it was right and proper to place that majestic gateway in a young woman's care.

THE SAINTE CHAPELLE

When we have turned the last pages of the last book of French history, there are two figures who stand out most clearly in our affections. They are not the figures of conquerors, though both took part in wars. They were not philosophers or moralists or great poets or scholars, though philosophy and scholarship and poetry sprung from them. They had little in common with the great and ornate figures who illuminate French history with their grand gestures and impeccable grammar; and there is even a sense in which these two figures are outside French history altogether, for they belong to legend and every man's love affair with the past. One of these figures was a king who resembled a monk, tall and willowy, with yellow hair flowing down to his shoulders and a perpetual smile hovering over his lips, the other was a dark-haired girl of eighteen or nineteen with a high forehead and a delicate heart-shaped face. One was Saint Louis and the other was Joan of Arc.

We know far more about Saint Louis who died before the walls of Carthage in 1270 than of Joan of Arc, who died in Rouen in 1431. We know his features and the shape of his mind and how he talked to his people and how deeply he loved them, and we would recognize him if he entered the room. We would perhaps recognize Joan of Arc from the two authentic portraits of her that remain, but she lived too briefly to enable us to penetrate the mysteries of her mind, so that even now, with all the documents at hand and a thousand books written about her, she remains elusive, and perhaps we love her all the more because she is almost beyond our understanding. Her voice was low and sometimes her judges had difficulty in hearing her, and we suffer from the same difficulty. There are moments when we see her clearly and other moments when she vanishes in the smoke of battle and the roaring of the flames.

On Saint Louis a steady light glows, and we see him clearly through all the years of his reign. All commentators are agreed upon his physical beauty, his easy grace of movement, his pallor, the sweetness of his smile. The stories told about him confirm the descriptions of his person. He liked the company of monks so much that he was sometimes called "Friar Louis." Once an old woman mocked him, calling him king of the monks, and swearing that he should be chased from the throne. He answered gravely: "In all you say you are telling the truth, for I am unworthy to be king. Our Lord, if He had been so minded, would have put a better person on the throne." He liked to dispense justice at Vincennes, sitting on the ground under an oak tree, and he would smile with amused tolerance if anyone contradicted him. One day he asked one of his companions: "Which would you rather be—a leper or in mortal sin?" "I would rather have committed thirty or forty sins than be a leper," the companion replied. The king said nothing, but the next day he summoned the man and said: "Come sit at my feet. Yesterday you spoke rashly, for all the ills of the body are cured in a little time when a man dies, but if the soul is tarnished and if you are uncertain whether God has pardoned you, the evil will last forever as long as God sits in Paradise." Then he asked the young man suddenly whether he ever washed the feet of poor men on Maundy Thursday, and the young man answered: "Sire, far be it from me to wash the feet of poor men! No! Never will I do such a thing!" The king said: "Then you are wrong again—thinking yourself too great to do what God did for our enlightenment. Now I pray you for the love of God and for the love of me, get yourself into the habit of washing poor men's feet." The king washed the feet of the poor, not as a penance, but because he was genuinely attached to the poor and wanted to honor them, and after kissing their feet, he would go on to carve their meat and cut their bread and then, when they had eaten, he would himself eat the scraps they had left on their plates. He would go to hospitals and work there like the commonest nurse, even to emptying the bedpans. In the Holy Land, after fighting the Saracens, he would help to bury the dead on the battlefield. "He himself carried the putrid and stinking corpses," wrote the chronicler Jean de Joinville, "and never once held his nose as the others did."

Though the king hated ostentation, and preferred to wear his dark brown taffeta tunic with a dark blue mantle of some coarse cloth over it, he was perfectly aware that the splendor of the court had to be maintained and he told his sons to dress well. "You should clothe yourselves well and decently," he said, "so that your women will love you more and your household will respect you; for the wise men say we ought to dress and arm ourselves in such a manner that neither shall the good men of the world blame us for extravagance nor the young blades for meanness." Following his own advice he would appear on ceremonial occasions in a sumptuous vermilion surcoat edged with ermine.

He was a man who walked all his life with an inner quietness, an inner certainty. He prayed incessantly, waking up at midnight to hear matins at the altar, and sometimes his knights would find him in a church with his knees on the bare pavements and his elbows on a bench, and when they reminded him there were important matters to attend to, he would look up with a perplexed smile and say: "Where am I?" Yet he was no peaceful monk hungry for devotions. He ruled France with determination and astuteness, and he was ferocious against his enemies. He led two Crusades against the Saracens. On a summer's day in 1249 he leaped fully armed from his flagship, the *Montjoye*, into the sea at Damietta and he would have attacked an army of six thousand infidels singlehanded if his knights had not prevented him. He died at the age of fifty-five on another Crusade, near Carthage, on another raging summer day, calling upon Saint Denis and Saint Geneviève, the patron saints of France and Paris, and among his last words was a prayer to his son: "Keep your heart soft and gentle to the poor, and the misshapen, and all who are ill at ease, and comfort and aid them within your power." Long before his death he had been regarded as a saint.

This man who loved quiet speech had a voice which can be heard across the centuries. That voice was too much his own to be characteristic of his age. His gaiety, his simple delight in being himself, his habit of speaking very simply and directly, yet sometimes with a directness which concealed an almost incredible cunning, his love of conversation, his furious courage, all these belong to his age; his determination to bring about a united France stretching from the channel to the Mediterranean and the Pyrenees belongs to a later time, and in this he was in advance of his age.

There is a small wooden statue of him which comes from the Sainte Chapelle and was made only a few years after his death. The arms are missing and some of the paint has flaked away, but the very essence of him is there as he stands in a dark rose-red gown gazing into the distance, his head bent forward a little in eagerness. The broad forehead, the widely set eyes, the long nose and wide sensitive mouth suggest the scholar, but if you look closely you can see, I think, the quivering devotion and deeply religious feeling and the grave assurance of a man who knows he is a king. It shows him about the age of twenty-five, when he received the Crown of Thorns from the Emperor Baldwin II of Constantinople and walked barefoot with the sacred treasure to Paris.

In the whole course of his life the king probably never knew such pure and intense excitement as when he made that eight-day journey from Villeneuve-l'Archevêque, where he received the treasure, to the Cathedral of Nôtre Dame, where it was temporarily deposited. It was August, 1239, and crowds thronged the road under the burning skies as the king marched at the head of the procession bearing the small wooden casket which contained two inner caskets, of gold and silver. Only the year before news had reached him that the Emperor Baldwin had borrowed vast sums of money from the Venetians, offering the Crown of Thorns as security, and was unable to repay the loans. The Crown of Thorns was in fact for sale. The king was overjoyed, and perfectly willing to pay any price for the possession of the Crown, and it never occurred to him to doubt the authenticity of the relic. He sent two Franciscans to Constantinople to make the purchase. The Crown was in a *coffre-fort* in the warehouse of Nicola Quirino, the leading Venetian merchant in Constantinople: the price was 177,300 livres, amounting to perhaps $4,000,000 of our money. A heavy down payment was made, and the Franciscans returned by slow stages to France. At Villeneuve-l'Archevêque, on the borders of Burgundy and France, the relic was solemnly received by the king and his brother Robert of Artois, and the journey to Paris began.

Two years later there came news that a large portion of the True Cross was for sale. Once again the king sent his emissaries. Once again he made the journey to the border to receive the relic and to carry it barefoot to Paris, and to show it to the assembled multitudes. Then he decided to build a chapel which would serve as a reliquary for the two treasures, to be known as *La Chapelle de la Sainte Couronne et la Sainte Croix.* No one knows the name of the architect who was employed to design the chapel, though it seems to have been Pierre de Montereau, already famous for his work at Saint Denis and the Lady Chapel of Saint Germain-des-Prés. Unlimited sums of money were placed at his disposal. The existing church of Saint Nicholas was knocked down, and in its place there rose in less than three years—from the summer of 1245 to the spring of 1248—a chapel like no other in Christendom, for it was made of thousands upon thousands of pieces of colored glass. When the sun emerges from behind a cloud, the chapel seems to throb and glow as though bathed in a stream of rainbows.

Even at Chartres there is nothing to compare with the massive jewel-like incandescence of the building which we know today as the Sainte Chapelle. Here light is triumphant, pouring through those immense windows like a benediction. Those scarlets and russet reds, the blazing yellows and cool blues combine to form a foretaste of Paradise as they move in slow waves from one wall to the other so that every fragment of the air is colored and as though radiant with divinity. Something of the same effect is achieved in the somber Capella Palatina in Palermo, when the candlelight flickers on the walls sheeted with glittering mosaics, but even the most luminous mosaics retain a kind of earthly heaviness. The Sainte Chapelle has no heaviness. It is as light as air, and more beautiful than any imaginable day in spring.

There is nothing in all Paris so perfect as this chapel erected by Saint Louis on the eve of the disastrous Seventh Crusade. Of the fifteen hundred square yards of painted glass, which seem to be barely supported by a thin framework of pillars, more than a thousand square yards of the original glass remain. The high altar has gone, and many of the relics accumulated by the king have vanished, but the chapel remains as a testimony to the king's adoration of Christ. It is not only that there is no other chapel like it, but no other is conceivable. It could have been built only by a king possessed of deep and overwhelming faith, prepared to squander the accumulated wealth of his kingdom in purchasing the relics and building a house worthy of them; and he could have built it only at a time when the making of stained glass windows had become an exacting art with great craftsmen working at it, and at a time when Gothic was youthful and in the ascendant. Such a dazzling triumph could have no imitators.

For the king the Sainte Chapelle was the dearest jewel in his crown. The king himself kept the keys of the great reliquary in which the relics were housed on a gilded platform above the high altar; and like a connoisseur of holy emblems he must add continually to his collection. He had already acquired the blade of the Holy Lance and the Holy Sponge when the Sainte Chapelle was dedicated. Within a decade he acquired the Nails, the Reed, the Purple Robe, a piece of the Holy Shroud, a portion of the Napkin used by Mary Magdalene to wash His feet, a phial of the Virgin's Milk and another of the Precious Blood, a stone from the Holy Sepulcher and the inscription which surmounted the Cross, together with the blue mantle of the Virgin and the swaddling clothes worn by Christ in the manger. In time he even acquired the Rod with which Moses struck the Rock, for there was no end to the inventiveness of the Byzantines and Venetians. It mattered little to him whether these relics could be authenticated; it was enough that they existed and that he could adore them bathed in the holy light pouring through the windows.

In time one final, authentic relic was added to the collection—the skull of Saint Louis himself, canonized within thirty years of his death. The skull was placed in the gilded and jeweled coffer which contained so many precious relics. It was perhaps an inevitable addition to the treasure, but it would have appalled him to know that his skull would rest there. "I must have no pride," he said once. "My task is to serve France humbly and decorously, and to that end I will bend all my remaining strength."

The Sainte Chapelle survived unharmed until the French Revolution. Then the mob poured in, and the gilded coffer vanished, and so did the statues of the twelve apostles lining the walls. Later, when an accounting was made, it was discovered that a few relics had survived: the Crown of Thorns was rescued, and so were the phial of the Precious Blood and the stone from the Holy Sepulcher, and they are now in the treasury of Nôtre Dame. Two of the statues of the apostles are in the Cluny Museum, and some of the jewels from the reliquaries in the Cabinet des Médailles. In the sixties of the last century a single sprig of the Holy Thorn was placed in the great ball of the remodeled spire. It would have pleased Saint Louis to know that some part of the Crown of Thorns he had received from the emperor of Constantinople floated high above Paris, presiding over the destiny of the city.

AIGUES-MORTES

On one of the hottest days of the year I walked across the edge of the Camargue from Les Saintes Maries to Aigues-Mortes. I remember the sky was an intense quivering blue, and there was a strange emptiness in the sky and in the salt plains where nothing grows. Here and there were small farms, set back from the winding dusty road, but in the heat of the day no one ventured forth. In that unrelenting heat the sound of footsteps came like drumbeats on the taut skin of the earth.

The Camargue is a treacherous place, and men have been known to see mirages and lose themselves among the salty wastes: a careful traveler will keep strictly to the road and resist the temptation to explore the barren hinterland. A mile from Les Saintes Maries, and you are in the desert, and this is strange, for the town with the great yellow fortified church has none of the appearance of a frontier town. On the contrary it is nearly always gay and sparkling, bathed in a wonderful clean light, full of women in vivid dresses, and with cattle men wearing white sombreros and dark-eyed fishermen fresh from their painted boats. When I think of Les Saintes Maries I remember the bustle of the market place, and the high yellow church, and the abandoned railroad car with its dark orchestra of mosquitoes where I once spent a night because the hotels were full, but most of all, as I grow older, I remember a small curving strip of shore with white boulders heaped on the sea's edge to prevent the sea from invading the land; and there was nothing remarkable about that scene except its quietness and peace, the sweetness of a curving bay, and the strange effect of the light glancing off the white rocks, so that there was a kind of fuming screen thrown up in front of the intense blue sea, and somehow this fuming from the white rocks gave a new dimension to the sea, making it seem remote and unreachable and even more beautiful. Behind the dazzling screen a red-sailed boat seemed to be wandering through a dream.

But there were no silvery screens of light pouring across the Camargue: only the relentless golden heat, the throbbing, the barren landscape, the taste of salt in the air. Once I saw a pink cloud glinting briefly on the horizon: it was a flight of flamingoes, but they soon settled among the salty wastes which are their home. It was shortly after I had seen the flamingoes that I realized I had lost my way. I could retrace my steps or go on, but it would make no difference. There were no houses in sight, no people. There were many roads wandering hither and thither across the plain, and one could be just as lost by following the roads as by wandering across the Camargue; and then it came to me that like many others I had probably been walking in circles.

The sun was directly overhead, a ball of golden flame in a sky which was no longer blue, but white-hot. The sensible thing, I thought, would be to take off my shirt and wrap it round my head; and this I did. The next thing was to sit down in the shade of a tree and try to work out a sense of direction, and this too I did, with no spectacular result, for with the plain stretching on all sides, and with the sun directly overhead, all directions were the same. Beyond a clump of gnarled olive trees there was a rise where the earth seemed to be greener, no longer parched and russet yellow and glaring white, and this I took to be the northwest. I had no map, but knew that Aigues-Mortes was somewhere in the northwest from Les Saintes Maries. So I abandoned the road and walked to the clump of olive trees, and was saved from spending the rest of my life wandering in the Camargue. One moment all seemed lost; the next moment I was striding down a wide asphalt road toward Aigues-Mortes, which ap-

peared some minutes later far away at the foot of low, rolling hills—
a white city with high walls, towers, parapets, a child's toy.

No one who has seen Aigues-Mortes will ever forget that first
glimpse of it. Aigues-Mortes means "the dead waters," but there is
nothing in the least sinister about the town. It is so splendidly medieval that it seems to be shouting and clapping its hands. It is exactly
like the towns you see in illuminated manuscripts, and it is more handsome than most, for the Tour de Constance, overlooking the canal
which runs along one side of the square town, is a marvel of grace
and power, and gives grace and power to the town. It is the color of
a gray egg shell, smooth and windowless except for long, narrow slits,
and it seems to have been designed by an architect determined to find
exactly the right proportions, marrying the tower to the long crenelated walls and the fourteen great gates.

Once Aigues-Mortes stood on the edge of the sea, and ships sailed
from its water gates to the Holy Land. Twice Saint Louis set sail from
here on ill-fated Crusades. The first time was in 1248, when he fitted
out thirty-eight ships and a vast assembly of weapons for an attack
on Egypt, guarding the right flank of the Holy Land. More than
twenty thousand men set out on the expedition, but only a handful
returned six years later. Saint Louis captured Damietta and then lost it
and was taken prisoner, to be ransomed for a million gold bezants.
From Aigues-Mortes too he set out on his last Crusade, this time
against the infidel king of Tunis. It took eighteen days for the small
fleet to cross the Mediterranean, and Saint Louis was already dying.
The African summer overwhelmed the Crusaders before they could
engage the enemy; thousands perished; and the French king became
the victim of the plague which had carried off so many of his soldiers.
He died, praying to Saint James, Saint Denis and Saint Geneviève,
on a bed of ashes, his hands crossed on his chest, looking up to
Heaven, "at the same hour," says the chronicler Joinville, "that the
Son of God died upon the cross for the world's salvation." Only two
months before he was busily provisioning his fleet at Aigues-Mortes.

Aigues-Mortes is always associated with Saint Louis, but in fact the
walled town scarcely existed in his day. For him it was nothing more
than a patch of land, a springboard within the domain of a foreign

prince. He built the Tour de Constance immediately after purchasing the land from the Abbot of Psalmody, and he may have constructed a few houses, but the walls as we see them today were built by his son, Philippe le Hardi. Aigues-Mortes lay within the kingdom of Provence and was not then in France.

Still, the Tour de Constance is his, and among the glories of his reign. It has an imperial grandeur, stern but outwardly not forbidding, calm and august, dominating the plain, with a characteristically French gentleness and an equally characteristic strength. The architecture inside is almost voluptuous: it might be a series of Gothic chapels with its carved capitals and finely groined vaulting. There are three such chapels, one on top of the other. Yet these vast chapel-like rooms are fortresses forming an almost impregnable bastion against an enemy. If the hostile forces succeeded in bursting into the lower chapel, they would be attacked from the one above it with arrows, stone balls and burning oil, and if they somehow forced their way into the second chapel, they would be faced with the same deadly shower of flames and projectiles. There were therefore three planned and deliberate lines of retreat. In the entire history of the tower there is no record that it was ever taken except by treachery. Other towers might be taken, but not the tower built by Saint Louis.

The tower of the Burgundians, built by his son, was taken several times, most notably in January, 1421, when a royal army crept stealthily under its walls. It was a bitterly cold, moonless night, and the Burgundian garrison had feasted well and taken to their beds, believing the royal army to be still far away. The royalists wrapped their feet in cloth and silently climbed the parapet. There were no sentinels; not a sound could be heard. Presently they found themselves outside the tower, and entered it as easily as you enter it today. The Burgundians awoke, but not for long. For about a quarter of an hour the massacre went on, until there was not one Burgundian left alive; and when the Baron de Vauverbe was asked what should be done with the bodies, he answered: "Let them rot there." The people of Aigues-Mortes were afraid of the pestilence from the decomposing bodies, and asked permission to salt the Burgundians. Permission was given. They went out to the salt lakes in the neighborhood and brought in enough salt to fill the tower. In ancient chronicles you will sometimes hear the phrase "salted Burgundians" in reference to catastrophic defeats. The contemporary chronicler was at pains to explain that there was nothing barbarous in the attitude of the people of Aigues-Mortes: they had acted solely for purposes of hygiene.

The tower of the Burgundians is a small and not very impressive tower, without the grace of the hundred-foot-high Tour de Constance. Only one legend attaches to the Burgundian tower: there are countless legends attached to the Tour de Constance, which from being a fortress palace became a prison. Here for over a century Protestants were taught the evil of their ways. At one time there were said to be a thousand Protestants in those three rooms. In 1767 the Prince de Beauvan, Governor of Languedoc, came to Aigues-Mortes on a mission of mercy. Here is the account of his secretary, de Boufflers, who accompanied the prince:

We found at the entry to the tower an eager guardian, who led us through a dark and twisting passage, and opened a great clanging door on which Dante's line might well have been inscribed: *Lasciate ogni speranza voi ch' entrate*. I have no colors in which to paint the terrors of the picture which gradually grew upon our unaccustomed eyes. The scene was hideous yet pathetic, and interest in its victims struggled with disgust at their condition. Almost without air and light, fourteen women languished in misery and tears within that stone-walled chamber. As the commandant, who was visibly touched, entered the apartment, they all fell down together at his feet. I can still see them, bathed in tears, struggling to speak, unable at first to do anything but sob. Encouraged by our evident sympathy they all began to tell us their sorrows at once. Alas, the crime for which they were then suffering was the fact that they had been brought up in the same religion as Henri IV. The youngest of them was fifty, and she had been here since she was eight years old. In a loud voice that shook with emotion the marshal said, "You are free!" and I was proud to be his servant at that moment.

The most famous of the prisoners he released was Marie Durand, who had spent thirty-seven years in the prison: a cheerful woman who kept up the spirits of the other prisoners with a stream of prayers and exhortations. It was perhaps Marie Durand who wrote in magnificent bold letters the word which can still be seen carved on the stone floor:

RESISTER. That word, in that place, has a fierce and troubling beauty, like a passion of the soul.

The Tour de Constance was the palace of a king, a fortress and a prison, and in all this it followed a perfectly normal evolution; but there is nothing normal in the delicacy of its lines, the calm assurance in the leaping thrust of the stone, the splendor of its outline. It is a Crusader's castle in miniature, devoid of ornament, completely functional, almost an abstraction. It must have been still more beautiful when it stood on the edge of the sea, before the fleet of the Crusaders sailed away and left it there, like the churches in Ravenna, forgotten in the marshlands.

Standing on the top of the tower, you can look down on the red roofs of the town arranged in orderly rows, and beyond the smoke-colored walls of Philippe le Hardi lie the salt flats in calm desolation, while here and there a glinting white pyramid of salt rises like a mockery of Egypt. Once all this region was a Roman granary, but now there is only a sense of desolation and emptiness, the end of the world. People walk very slowly in Aigues-Mortes. They are in no hurry. They have seen empires rise and fall, and they have learned patience.

CARCASSONNE

It is best to come to Carcassonne in the afternoon, when the long shadows are falling—those shadows which are the color of purple grapes—and to take one's time climbing up to the old battlemented city which stands on a hill, looking down on the modern city with its roar of traffic and crowded department stores, with the smell of gasoline everywhere. The old city is a miracle of blue roofs and pointed turrets and medieval archways, and even the dull biscuit-colored walls, which hold the sunlight, seem perfectly appropriate as they look down upon the River Aude, that sluggish, weed-choked river which is the boundary between the new and the old. Beyond the river lies the vision of a medieval paradise, or a child's happy toy —the banners are flying, and the drawbridge is being lowered to receive the king's envoys, and very soon there will be war with the Saracens, and gunpowder and machine guns and atom bombs lie far in the future.

There are still walled cities to be found all over France: there is even one, Provins, not sixty miles from Paris. Only Aigues-Mortes can rival Carcassonne, but Aigues-Mortes lies on a plain, and is much smaller even with its great tower, which is perhaps the most beautiful tower in all Europe. Carcassonne is beautiful in another way—in the sheer majesty of its position, in the wonderful silhouettes of crenelated walls, with so many turrets and forts and pinnacles that it convinces by sheer multiplication. They will tell you that more than half of Carcassonne is a restoration by Viollet-le-Duc, and so it is, but it hardly matters. Viollet-le-Duc took the ruined bones, poured marrow into them, and gave them flesh. If you look too closely at Carcassonne the illusion will vanish, but if you stand at the first arch of the seven-arched bridge and look straight at the hill, the illusion is complete. There she is, blue-robed and immaculate, and there is no lovelier city anywhere than this ghostly city set against the heavens.

She is so beautiful from the bridge that there is something to be said for going no farther. On closer view she is patched and painted, and she wears her finery with the air of an old strumpet pretending to be young again, slapping powder on her cheeks for fear we shall see the pox and the wrinkles. Still, even now she is elegant, and she wears well. The lords of Trencavel, who once lived there, would not be ashamed of her.

Even now the old city of Carcassonne somehow suggests the frontier. Once the River Aude, little wider than a ditch, was the frontier of France, with the counts of Barcelona ruling to the west. The city has the brazenness of a frontier post, which must be especially embellished to impress the enemy lurking on the other side of the river, and the massive fortifications were constructed with an eye to displaying power as much as to employing power. Seeing the city from a distance we are impressed with its gentleness, imagining the quiet traffic within the walls and the sense of enduring safety which comes from being so well guarded, but in the Middle Ages Carcassonne was a nervous, chattering place, full of alarms and excursions, quick to arms whenever a shadow appeared on the plain. There were fifty-two towers, but only four thousand people in the city. Most of the women seemed to have lived in tents outside the city walls, and they were allowed in the walls, if they were allowed at all, only if the enemy was at the gates. As long as it was a frontier post, Carcassonne was stripped bare for fighting.

This is not quite the picture presented by the French movies, which are nearly always filmed at Carcassonne whenever there is any need of battlements and drawbridges. In these movies the knights-at-arms, the pretty heroines and the peasants are always immaculately clothed, and carefully washed behind the ears. The grubbiness of the Middle Ages is notably absent. The dirt, the squalor, the foul smell of hay which has lain too long on the floors, the running sores, the open drains, the armies of the misshapen, the lame, the wounded and the tortured, all this is absent. The lord had his spacious castle, and the bishop had his palace, but for everyone else there were only cramped stifling quarters. In one of the bastions of Carcassonne is the room where the Inquisitors examined and sometimes tortured the heretics: the room is a circle ten feet broad. One might have thought the Inquisitors would have been permitted to set up shop in a small corner of the church of the Bishop's palace.

They called Carcassonne "the Maiden," for once she had fallen into the possession of the King of France she remained impregnable. The city is an almost classic example of a fortress in depth, with every stratagem of the attacker anticipated by the designer. Nothing was left to chance. The outriding towers served as warehouses for supplies, and the slit windows permitted a merciless crossfire on the attackers attempting to scale the walls. Flying balconies were provided with holes through which boiling oil could be poured on the attackers, and slots through which boulders could be let fall. The fortress was like a complicated mouse trap. The attackers would batter down the gates and find themselves in a kind of hallway already deep within the fortress; then at each end of the hallway the portcullises would descend, trapping them, leaving them to the mercy of boiling oil, flaming tar, arrows and iron bolts, and if these were insufficient to quell their spirits there was always a convenient supply of boulders to crush their bones. And if the outer wall was breached, and all its forts captured, there remained the inner *enceinte*, a tiny fortified city built around the lord's palace, high-walled and booby-trapped, for the weary attackers to assault, and within this stood the barbican where the last-ditch fight was fought. No wonder Carcassonne was impregnable! The defense had long since outstripped attack, so that it became customary to assume that the attackers would lose ten men for one of the defenders. Such logistics tend to make generals delay their assaults as long as possible.

There is a pleasant story, dating from the Middle Ages, which tells how Carcassonne was attacked by the vast armies of Charle-magne. The Saracen King Balaak made a last desperate sortie, only to be captured and strangled for refusing to embrace the Christian faith. His wife, the Lady Carcas, fought on until there were only a handful of survivors left, and as the siege continued even these survivors per-ished of famine. The Lady Carcas quickly set about making straw puppets, which she propped up in all the towers, and she ran from one tower to another firing off arrows, giving the impression of an army. There was almost no food left, but she had the sense to stuff a pig with the remaining wheat, and then she cut the pig's throat and tossed it over the walls, where it burst open. The burst pig was brought to Charlemagne, who came to the conclusion that the army defending the city was well provisioned and would hold off the siege for another five years if need be. So he gave orders to raise the siege, and he led his troops northward. He was already marching away when he saw a wild woman running out of the city and madly ringing a bell to attract his attention. She was recognized and all the soldiers shouted: "*Carcas sonne*"—"Carcas is ringing her bell!" And soon she was sur-rendering her city and herself to Charlemagne, and being baptized, and a husband was found for her, and so she became the mother of the Earl of Trencavel.

Unhappily for the medieval legend, the name of Carcassonne is in no need of a romantic explanation. Long before the Lady Carcas emerged from her fortress ringing a bell, the Romans called it Carcaso, and they gave the gentle River Aude the ferocious name of Atax. For five and a half centuries, from 118 B.C. to A.D. 440, the Romans had their fortified camp on the hill, until it fell before the armies of the Visigoths; and it pleases the people of Carcassonne to believe that their city was the last resting place of Alaric, King of the Goths, who was buried, they say, in the nearby Mont Aric together with all the treasure of Rome and Athens, the marble sculptures and the golden sheeting from the Temple of Jupiter Capitolinus and the seven-branched candlestick from Jerusalem and all the rest of that fabulous wealth which represented the inheritance of three civilizations. The treasure of Alaric has vanished, and no trace of it has ever been found; and on Mont Aric no one has discovered even a gold hairpin.

But it is not of Romans, Goths and Saracens that you find yourself thinking when you walk through the streets of Carcassonne or along the battlements. There is the feeling that at any moment the curtain will be lifted, and those empty streets and battlements will suddenly be crowded with wild, long-haired men in armor speaking a language which is richer and more violent than the French spoken today. The illusion of being in the past is very nearly complete. Viollet-le-Duc did his work well. French scholars have told me that blue slate tiles were never used in the Middle Ages, and instead those pepperbox turrets were faced with the same red tiles you see on all the neighboring farmhouses. It may be so. But no one entering the old town of Carcassonne would dream of having it otherwise.

But the jewel of Carcassonne lies deep within the fortifications. This is the small Romanesque cathedral of Saint Nazaire with its Gothic chapels built by Pierre de Rochefort, with a wonderful array of stained glass windows. There is nothing overwhelming about the cathedral. It is quiet and chaste, very airy, with an amazing purity of line, so that you find yourself reminded of the spiritual mood of the great cathedrals of northern France. The rose windows do not paint the air, but give a subtle tint to the airy arcades where the worshipers wander; there is no fierce splendor of color as at Chartres, no blaze of jeweled light, only a gentle and steady refulgence. In the cool northern rose, all green and violet, the Virgin is attended by censing angels. The south rose is warmer, with orange and scarlet, depicting Christ in majesty, and the colors glow like small flames in an awakening fire. Yet it is the Tree of Jesse which dominates the cathedral, and this immense window, with its scarlet tree winding across the glass like a river on an ancient map, scatters the light into little jeweled filaments of color. Nothing quite like this tree exists anywhere else in France: that softness, that delicacy are not to be found in the north, where the light is less intense. Craftsmen from Toulouse made this glass in the fourteenth century, and they seem to have deliberately put the pieces together to give an effect of calm, a quiet radiance, like the light glittering from a tree-shaded river in the setting sun.

The Cathedral of Saint Nazaire can best be compared with the

Sainte Chapelle. It does not, like the Sainte Chapelle, leap with exultation, but it possesses the same deliberate and controlled simplicity, the
same rounded severity of form. Instead of joy there is peace.

So, wandering through the streets of Carcassonne, climbing some of
those seven thousand stairs and entering some of the fifty towers en-
circling the ancient city, one returns again and again to this quiet
place bathed in a cool light, the jewel at the heart of the fortress.
Here the medieval dream reaches a triumphant conclusion: here the
sanctuary of the Grail is defended by the great battlements of Sarras.

AIX-EN-PROVENCE

There is a story told by Chrétien de Troyes in the twelfth century of a young and handsome knight meeting a peasant "who had the eyes of an owl, the nose of a cat, and the teeth of a wild boar." The peasant was leaning on a club, dressed only in skins, surly and uncommunicative, so ugly and dark visaged that at first the young knight was not sure whether he was human and rode up to him in the manner of a man ready to attack an evil thing. Then they confronted one another, neither speaking, and the knight found himself wondering whether any words would ever come from that strange animal's mouth. "What are you?" asked the knight, and the peasant answered: "I am a man."

I would think of that peasant when wandering over France, for he is still there, a hard, strange, uncommunicative, determined person, so much in love with his land that he seems to be a part of it. He is of the earth, earthy. He knows the seasons and the sky and the roots of things. He believes that life goes on, that when he dies a child will be born to carry on the work of the land. He believes in the fertility of the earth, and there is no other belief which satisfies him so completely. He knows that France is indestructible because the earth is so rich, and he is content with his knowledge.

I think of my Uncle Julien, over eighty, red-faced and fat as a barrel, as he stomps through his orchards in the little village of Côte d'Arey near Vienne, and with every gesture he proclaims his sense of community with the earth. Once he asked me to help him gather the pears, and I went about plucking the pears in what I thought was a thoroughly sensible way. Then he came up stealthily and watched me with a look of pity, until he could control himself no longer. "It's all wrong," he said. "You should lift the pear gently in the palm of your hand until the stem breaks, and do it gently." He said "*doucement, doucement*" over and over again, smiling, showing me how it should be done, his enormous feet planted solidly in the earth, caressing the pear like a lover.

Most of all I envied his proud sense of possession, or rather of being possessed by the earth he owned. I have watched him at dusk stooping down and gathering clods of earth in his worn hands, and gazing at the clods as though daring them to speak; and when he let the earth fall back again, he would always do it gently. He drank wine by the bucketful, ate like a trencherman, roared out commands at the top of his lungs, and hugely enjoyed being mayor of the village, which is so small that I have never seen it marked on a map. At night, when the earth is quiet, he would stand by the door of his house and look with a puzzled expression at the dark land. "Well, the earth must sleep too," he would say, and in his voice and intonation there was the unmistakable realization that the earth was a living thing. One day at dusk I stood beside him while the ghostly white cattle were coming up the slope past the village church. "Watch," he said. "They will stop by the church. Didn't you know that the cattle also pray?" He was laughing quietly, and when the cattle came to the gates of the church, mysteriously white and silent in the dusk, they paused and for a few moments it seemed that they were praying. Then they ambled down the village street and were lost in the darkness.

I used to think that no one had ever depicted the French peasant in his glory. There are plenty of novels describing him, but they seem to miss his pride, his self-assurance, his calm defiance, all those elements which were noted by Chrétien de Troyes when he made the peasant say: "I am a man." They miss his religious devotion to the land. I wondered why he was so rarely depicted through the centuries, until it occurred to me that he was almost beyond the reach of words. Only one man has depicted the French peasant successfully, and that was Cézanne, not in words but in paint, and not in portraits but in his way of looking at the earth. If you look at Cézanne's paintings, you will see how the earth appears to a peasant of the south of France.

Cézanne's studio is still standing on the hills above Aix, near Entremont. He built it in the winter of 1901 out of the money he inherited from his father. From his house in Aix he would come every morning to the studio on the Chemin de Lauves, from where he could look out on his beloved Mont Sainte Victoire, and if he turned in another direction he could look out on the red roofs of Aix. The studio, with its immense northern window, has changed very little since he left it. The relics are here. His green cloak, his battered straw hat, the thick leather hunting bag which he took with him on his excursions, his easel, palette and paint brushes, even the dry tubes of paint are all here. Here, too, is the familiar blue-and-white ginger jar which can be seen in many of his paintings. There is a black crucifix on the wall, jugs, chairs, wine glasses, flowerpots, a profusion of objects worth nothing at all, though his painting of them is worth hundreds and thousands of dollars. Into one wall is cut the narrow slit which permitted him to bring into the studio the enormous canvases on which he painted his *Bathers* with increasing exasperation and fury. And here, too, on a shelf, are his skulls. They are brown and many of them are soft to the touch.

Cézanne was continually painting skulls. He would put a skull against a ginger jar, and paint them together: the jar quivering with life, and the skull receding into the darkness of the background. It is odd that he should have loved skulls so much, since he had such a fondness for the flesh of apples.

There are seven skulls in the studio, and I am told they are only a small part of the collection he formed. One would have thought one would be enough. Why seven? Is it possible that in some mysterious way he was influenced by the headhunters of Entremont, which is only a few yards away. He was nearly always alone in the studio— alone, and surrounded by skulls.

There is a clue perhaps in one of Cézanne's early poems, which he called "A Terrible Story." In this poem a poet is summoned by a

mysterious woman, the most beautiful he had ever seen. He throws
himself before her, kisses her breast, and on that very instant the chill
of death seizes him: the woman in his arms is changed to a corpse, a
rattling skeleton. The terror is real. The poem is a precise account of
a continuing nightmare which gripped him at intervals throughout his
life. Mortality was his companion, death his accomplice, and fear was
everywhere. "How fearful life is!" he was constantly saying. Fifteen
years before his death, he wrote to his son: "I feel that I have only a
few days left on earth—and then what? I believe I shall survive and
do not want to risk roasting *in eternum*." So we find him regularly
attending mass at the Cathedral of Saint Sauveur, and cursing priests,
torn between a pagan joy in life and a sorrowing fear of the after
life. Perhaps he painted skulls and lived with them because this was
the simplest, the most immediate method of encountering death and
wrestling with it.

We understand his paintings better when we remember "A Terrible Story" and the soft brown crumbling skulls which decorated his
studio, for all the world as though he were a Borneo headhunter. He
feared the transitory, and went in search of permanence. He would
embrace the goddess in such a way that the very violence of the
embrace would somehow make her permanent. He painted Mont
Sainte Victoire, so that it would endure. Van Gogh said of Cézanne
that he painted "the hard side of Provence," and this is true, but he
made the hard harder. His planes have the solidity of marble, and his
trees are rocks. For him the virtues of the living world were incom-
parably less than the virtues of the ideal, lucid, rock-hewn world of
his imagination. His earth is tough because it is the peasant's earth,
and like the peasant Cézanne was obsessed with the enduring and the
eternal.

I spent so long in the studio that the cheerful guardian quite properly wondered whether I had come to steal some of the surviving
paint brushes, or a skull, or the green jacket where a spider was
crawling. The sun came through the wide windows, flooding the
room with a soft orange light. In the calm of the studio it was strange
to think of Cézanne wrestling here alone with his angels.

They told stories after he died of how he was heard shouting at the top of his lungs in a furious rage against the canvas or the paint. Once he fell down in a dead faint, and was not discovered for many hours. He was always at boiling point, suffered from diabetes, feared women, hated noise and was happiest alone: he was surly, proud, miserly, and capable of acts of extraordinary generosity. Once he declared: "There is only one living painter—myself!"

In the last years of his life it was his custom to follow an unchanging ritual. In the early hours of the morning a hired carriage would come to fetch him at his house in Aix. The carriage was a very old one, beautifully upholstered in red velvet, with a faded coat of arms on the door, and the springs creaked loudly. It was drawn by two old white horses. He would be taken to his studio in the hills and left there, alone except for the gardener who came irregularly. So it was, and so it would always be, until he died.

Early in October, 1906, the old coachman who had served him for so long demanded an increase of wages. There was a stormy interview, and Cézanne refused to pay the sum demanded. Then, every morning, he walked up to the studio alone and every evening he took the long winding road back to Aix. The morning of October 13 was sunny. He spent most of the morning painting his gardener, Vannier, in the garden, and after lunch, following his custom, he set out to paint in the countryside near Entremont. He was still painting when a violent storm sprang up. He tried to walk back to the studio, but the storm was too much for him and he collapsed on the roadside, where he was found some hours later, drenched through and suffering from fever, by the driver of a laundry cart. He was carried back to Aix, and it took two men to put him in bed.

Surprisingly, on the next morning, he felt sufficiently well to resume his painting, and slipped out of the house and made his way to the studio, where he added a few touches to the painting of the gardener. But the effort was too much for him. This time he returned to Aix in a neighbor's carriage, and he never went to the studio again. He had hoped to die painting in the open fields; instead he died in his bed of double pneumonia.

The old peasant died long ago, but even now the studio is full of him. You have the feeling that he might walk in at any moment, a

small, choleric, sharp-nosed man with a goatee and a broad-brimmed
hat stuck firmly on his head, growling to himself as he prepares oil and
paint and canvas and roaring at the top of his voice when anything
went wrong. He had a thick southern accent: it was so thick an accent that people in Paris could scarcely understand him. So for a while
he would rage at the canvas, but afterward he would settle down into
a calm, which was like a truce between opposing armies. He was
devilishly proud, and knew it. Once he said: "We should all be
humble before the sun, which gives us such beautiful light."

TOULOUSE

Aix-en-Provence still wears the air of a village. Though it has Renaissance palaces by the score and at least ten churches and the memory of its ancient kings is still fresh in people's minds, it gives the impression of being in a quiet backwater. The Cours Mirabeau, the long tree-shaded street which lies at its heart, is a village highway. There is no hurry. People sit in the cafés, content to watch the world passing by. They have the enviable gift of being at peace with themselves.

Twenty years ago, when I first went to Toulouse, it seemed to me that I had never known a quieter town. It lived tranquilly in the backwaters, feeding on its past, but all this has changed. Today it is nearly as dangerous to cross a street in Toulouse as to cross a street in Paris. Jet planes are now made in Toulouse: it has become a vast and hectic metropolis. Wandering down familiar roads, which had suddenly grown unfamiliar, I thought I was in Barcelona. Toulouse has set its eyes against the past, and become a modern city.

Nîmes and Béziers and Carcassonne and Arles still sleep, but Toulouse is now wide awake, roaring at the top of its lungs. The steam hammers chatter away, and the riveting machines clatter, and the noise is insufferable. Recently, when the main streets were torn up to put in new drains, the city looked like a battlefield. It was then, I think, that I realized that the days of the troubadours and the Counts of Toulouse were finally over.

Still, there are pleasant retreats and gardens, and the Garonne is a charming river. There is excellent food, and what is far more important, a whole street of bookshops. Montauban and Moissac are nearby, the Pyrenees are only a few hours away by rail, and there is a fast train which will take you to Albi in an hour to see a cathedral which is the color of pink icing, if you like cathedrals the color of pink icing. But the chief treasures of Toulouse are still the Musée des Augustins and the basilica of Saint Sernin, and each has one jewel of formidable proportions. The jewel in the museum is the terra cotta statue of the Virgin made about 1550, but evidently continuing the tradition of the ancient Greek mosaic which showed Venus rising from the sea amid her curtained rainbows: exquisite, impudent, with the bloom of youth still on her. This Virgin is imperious, as a thirteen-year-old child is imperious; there is in her expression more than a hint of petulance. She is human and innocent and proud, and she is truly the Virgin. She too is hidden away in a dark corner, but shines most radiantly.

Henry James spoke of "the extraordinary seriousness" of the interior of Saint Sernin, but this is an understatement. Saint Sernin is a heavy weight on the soul. Though it was intended to rival the great cathedral in Santiago de Compostela, and every artifice was employed to produce a great church, something went wrong. The proportions are perfect, but it smells of the graveyard. It is fine, horribly fine, and leaves one cold. Compare it with Chartres or Moissac, and it produces an effect of total unwearying dullness. It has no grace, no simplicity, no lightness. Perhaps, after all, the learned Viollet-le-Duc put his finger on the heart of the matter when he observed that Saint Sernin was architecturally the most exact of churches, being based on a system of equilateral and right-angled isosceles triangles. Mathematical accuracy has only succeeded in destroying the spirit of the church.

But if the church itself is horrible, this is nothing to the horrors which await you in the Gothic crypt below the choir. There is an inscription on the wall which must make one pause:

NON EST IN TOTO SANCTIOR ORBE LOCUS
HIC SUNT VIGILES QUI CUSTODIUNT CIVITATEM

It is, of course, a boast of quite extraordinary magnitude. How one wishes it were true that one had come to the most sacred place in the world into the presence of those who keep vigil over our civilization! How one wishes it, and how quickly one's hopes are dispersed! For down below, in the dankness of the crypt, there is only a butcher's shop.

Portions of fifty saints are here, among them those who have the greatest title to sanctity. Charlemagne is supposed to have donated pieces of the six apostles Philip, Simon, Barnabas, Jude, James the Greater and James the Lesser. They are crated in great bronze coffers which may very well date from the time of Charlemagne. But this is only the beginning. There is the head of Saint Thomas Aquinas, a mottled brown skull wrapped in a faded napkin and exhibited in a glass case. There are pieces of Saint George of England, Saint Agatha, Saint Vincent de Paul, Saint Scholastica, Saint Suzanne of Babylon, Saint Papoul, Saint Edmund, who was king of England, and Saint Guillaume, who was duke of Aquitaine. All these relics are exhibited in a state of indescribable confusion, the glass cases jammed with bones and teeth and polyps of hideously aging flesh. The eye cannot rest, and the ears are monotonously assaulted by the toneless chanting of a surly guide, the custodian of custodians. There is only one relic of indisputable authenticity, and this is the strip of Byzantine silk with long-tailed birds derived from a Persian design in which Saint Louis received the Crown of Thorns. But the guide will not let his weak lamp shine on the silk for long. He is too busy pointing out the merits of incongruous bits of bone.

This butcher's shop, this chamber of horrors, has little to commend it. The smell of the grave and of death hangs over it: the glass tubes and gilded reliquaries have not been hermetically sealed. One staggers from one horror to another, while the echo of the guide's mournful voice wanders forlornly along the walls. It is a relief to come out of the cellar into the mathematical church again.

Saint Sernin is not wholly unrewarding, for in a corner of the north transept, so badly lit that it is almost invisible, stands the only crucifix of hammered bronze to survive from Romanesque times. It is life size and glows darkly, a figure of commanding power. There is no trace here of sorrow or of loving confidence, no tears, no wounds. Wide-eyed and thickly bearded, he looks out upon the world with majestic calm, conscious of his powers, for the crucifix is his throne and at any moment he will descend to earth or vanish in a blaze of fire to heaven. All the roughnesses, all the anatomical weaknesses of Romanesque art have somehow conspired to create a figure of heroic grandeur; and very oddly, and yet understandably the unknown sculptor has carved for the waistband supporting the loincloth an intricate jeweled clasp such as might be worn by a warrior-king in heroic times. Once there were jewels in the clasp, and perhaps there were jewels in the eyes. There must have been a time when this great crucifix looked down from a great height on the worshipers below, for it was the practice in France as in Italy to suspend the crucifix from the roof, producing an effect of overwhelming grandeur and domination. Those days are over, or nearly over. Today the bronze Christ lies hidden and forgotten in a corner, to emerge in the fullness of time.

LES BAUX

The rocks come out of the ground, and there are only ruins now—rock like flowing lava, rock hollowed into gaping tombs and quarries, rock bent and twisted as though a maniac had sprawled there and chosen to shape the rock into ultimate meaninglessness. Once there were palaces: now there are only the broken litter and the slow falling of stones into the valley below. Time and the winds have taken Les Baux by the throat and squeezed the last drop of blood from it.

Why then does one go there? Or, more precisely, why is it so exhilarating to wander among those bloodless ruins, that landscape with as many craters as the moon? Les Baux is high up and looks down on the great salt-marsh meadows of the Camargue, and the wind is pure, and the eagles circle overhead, but one does not go there to breathe the pure air. One goes, quite simply, to enjoy a landscape in its ultimate desolation and to see what happens when history comes to an end. Les Baux is the last act of a morality play.

It is an easy and pleasant journey from Aix through the sunlit olive fields, the air sparkling and the earth so richly colored that we seem to be traveling through a painting, for little has changed since Cézanne and Van Gogh painted it. The earth is strong and tender, and a golden swelling light flows over the olive trees, and Mont Sainte Victoire is never far away. Here, if anywhere, is a land fit for men to wander in and make love and enjoy the fruit of their labor, a land so calm and

rich and fruitful that one comes to envy the peasants who spend their
lives in these fields with something of the envy one has for the ancient
Greeks, for they seem to possess a grace which is denied to us. In
these calm fields the strong and tender sun falls like a blessing.

And then quite suddenly and unexpectedly, for there is nothing in
the contours of the earth to suggest the horror about to come, Paradise
gives way to Hell. The gentle fields become savage rocks, gnarled and
twisted teeth, naked bone splinters, strangely shaped blue-gray protuberances with an evil look about them. There is a queer molten
vigor about these rocks pushing up through the tender crust of the
earth. The sun flashes fiercely off these rocks, and there is no longer
the sense of blessing. Venomous, thrusting, strangling one another,
they pile upon one another like the bones of prehistoric beasts with
tatters of flesh still clinging to them; and they are the color of the
dark fires below the earth. They proclaim the existence of a world
outside history altogether.

Driving through these uprooted mountains, you have a foretaste
of what is to come. This is a landscape such as Dante may have remembered when he came to write about the circles of Hell, and indeed there is an ancient tradition that he passed along this road on
his way to Paris. The sense of a landscape in anguish and fearful tur-
moil does not leave you until you come at last to the soaring cliff
edge of Les Baux, from where you can look over the salt marshes to
the distant sea. The rocky fastness of Les Baux is only one more improbable naked fist thrown out of the tortured earth, larger and more
threatening than the rest.

On this naked fist the ancient lords of Les Baux built their fortresses and palaces. They were not the first to settle there, for the
Ligurians before them had already honeycombed the rock, and because
the Ligurians traded with the Greek colonists in Marseilles, and were
perhaps conquered by them, Corinthian helmets and Greek coins
have been found among the ruins. But of the Ligurians, those strange
wanderers over northern Italy and southern France, little is known.
We know more about the feudal lords who established themselves
among these cliffs during the tenth century, claiming descent from
the Magus Balthazar, and painting on their banner a silver star with

sixteen rays upon a field of gules to represent the star of Bethlehem. It was a strange and troubling device, and their violence was underscored by a more troubling inscription below the star:

A L'AZARD

BAUTEZAR!

meaning that the family of Balthazar was determined to hazard everything on conquest.

They were "a race of eagles, never vassal," as Mistral wrote, and the tortured rock of Les Baux was the eyrie where these young eagles nested in proud isolation. No one knows where they came from, though they seem to have come from beyond the sea, and it is possible that they were descended from a chieftain called Balthe who fought in the army of Uric, king of the Visigoths. By the tenth century they were rulers of all the plains to the north and south. They were the lords of the Camargue and the seacoast, and their will was law as far north as Orange and Vaucluse, and even Arles owed them fealty. Their strength lay in the rock, for they were unassailable. They gave themselves many titles, but it was the name "Bautezar" which inspired fear and obedience; and when they were weary of conquering the territories to the north, they fitted out ships along the estuaries of the Camargue and resorted to piracy.

From the beginning they were determined to rule by the sword, and soon we find them building a vast network of castles. Seventy-nine of these castles remain, though in ruins, but at least a hundred are known to have existed. These castles were not simply guard posts, but great concentrations of power, all of them flying the banner with the terrible sixteen-rayed star. Provence under their rule became a small kingdom. By 1215 Guillaume des Baux was permitted by the Holy Roman Emperor to call himself King of Arles and Vienne. Not long afterward another lord of Les Baux made himself briefly Emperor of Constantinople.

They were a turbulent family, high-spirited and a little mad. One of the lords of Les Baux was stabbed in prison by his wife, another besieged the castle of his niece when she was with child and deliberately undermined her chamber, and a third was flayed alive outside the walls of Avignon. They encouraged the troubadours and held their Courts of Love on the great rock, and there is a legend that after the husband of Berangère des Baux slew the great troubadour poet Guillen de Cabestanh, he cut out the poet's heart and presented it to his wife. She drank the blood and ate the meat before he told her where they came from. "So sweet is that meat and so pure the wine that none other shall pass my lips," she declared, and then she ran to the highest cliff and threw herself over the edge. So much may be legend, but the wine that grows beneath the highest cliff is still called Sanh del Trobador.

The legends, of course, proliferated; the very air was legendary. They called themselves the "comet" race, and took care to leave a trail of violence wherever they passed. And when at last in the autumn of 1426 Alix des Baux, the last of her race, lay dying, it was credibly reported that an enormous silver star with sixteen rays hovered gently above her head, vanishing only with her last breath.

One can believe anything about Alix, who succeeded to the sovereignty at the age of seven and waited patiently for twenty-six years before she could take up residence in her castle. Provence was at the mercy of the Vicomte de Turenne, who married her off to a young nobleman, Adon de Villars, in the hope that she would forget her inheritance. She never forgot. She swore on her marriage night, when she was thirteen, that she would regain her possessions. She intrigued with the Pope and the King of France, she raised armies, she sent embassies all over Europe. Turenne sacked the castle on Les Baux and threw everything in it over the cliffs. Alix never yielded. Her husband died, her friends deserted her, but she continued to fight. One day a messenger came with news that Turenne had accidentally drowned while crossing the Rhône. She did not wait for confirmation of the message, but set out immediately for her ruined castle, and there she remained for the next twenty-four years in contented luxury. No one dared to attack her, for the terror of her name still cast a spell on her enemies.

When Alix died, the good King René of Provence, who inherited her lands by right of being the most powerful contender for them, made an inventory of her estate. He found her palace crammed with gold and silver plate, oriental carpets, prayer books bound in gold leaf and set with pearls, a vast collection of jewel-studded liturgical plate. There were oaken chests overflowing with robes of silk and cloth of gold. There were tapestries illustrating the coming of the Magi, with her illustrious ancestor Balthazar in the foreground bending over the Christ child. There were galleries filled with armor, and it was noted on the inventory that the swords had grown rusty. Alix lived well from the profit of her lands and the great herds of sheep which grazed in the lowlands. King René stripped her castle bare and hastened to remove the finest of her possessions to his castle in Tarascon.

Soon all Provence and Les Baux with it passed into the hands of the king of France, who destroyed the battlements raised by King René and thought he had destroyed forever the power of the rock. Fifty years later we find François I making a royal progress through Provence and being entertained there by his own High Constable, Anne de Montmorency, to whom he had given the barony of Les Baux. Sometime later we hear of the Duc de Guise making another royal progress. The Duc commanded that a cannon should be fired every time he drank a toast, and having drunk many toasts he announced his intention of firing the gun himself. So he did, and the gun exploded, and he was buried at Saint Trophime in Arles.

Violence clung to the rock. The Protestants captured it, sacked the castle, set the furniture on fire, and went on to destroy the nearby church of Saint Catherine. Les Baux became the refuge of heretics and of all those who opposed the king of France. At last the Cardinal de Richelieu grew weary of the hornet's nest and ordered an end to it. The army moved up to the walls, a few shots were fired, and the citadel surrendered. "The fortress must be utterly destroyed," wrote the cardinal. There was no glamour in its destruction, no great fires, no savage fighting. By the cardinal's orders a troop of master masons from Tarascon was employed to reduce the fortifications brick by brick. With picks and hammers they reduced the eagle's nest to rubble.

Today it is still rubble and you can barely make out the ground plan of the palace of Alix des Baux. According to King René's inventory there were thirty-five rooms in the palace and the tower where she died was built over an immense granary which could have kept the entire population of Les Baux alive through a two years' siege. There is a single tumbledown street full of shops selling postcards, and two churches and perhaps eight or nine houses which may have existed in the time of King René. For the rest there is only an endless desolation of sterile rock gleaming like bones.

Les Baux is dead like the moon, and strangely exhilarating. It has been destroyed so many times that it wears the appropriate face of destruction. Its pride has been humbled in the dust and there is not even the faintest air of protest in the ruins. The Roman Forum cries out to rise again, but Les Baux cries only to be allowed to sleep in peace.

It would sleep more peacefully if there were not so many visitors crowding up the narrow street, and then, growing weary of the steep climb, crowding down again. The best is half a mile away, where the rock slopes steeply upward to the cliff edge, overlooking the Camargue and the salt meadows and the distant sea. Here the pure winds come in from the sea and the air is sweet and there is no sign of the ruins—only the emptiness of space and the illusion of being lifted to a vast height. Arles and the silver Rhône lie far below, and the villages seem no more than heaps of white pebbles. This steep rock has magic in it, for you find yourself pushed to the very edge of the cliff in order to see the vast landscape stretching below. The tug and pull of the rock cannot be easily fought. You lean on the wind, and if you fall, there is a drop of five hundred feet to the Sanh del Trobador. The wind howls in your ears, and the starlings fling themselves madly from one side of the cliff to the other, filling the air with their whistling and chattering, and there is so much exaltation in the air that you are dizzy with the excitement of gazing out over vast regions of space. Here at the cliff edge, far from the ruined walls, some of the secrets of Les Baux reveal themselves. You cannot look down from this high place for long without a feeling of domination and possession. All those plains stretching to the sea's rim seem to belong to

you. The very shape of the rock, the very shape of the plains somehow suggest mastery: and if you stayed on this edge of rock the lust
of conquest, the eagle's eye, would be born in you.

That afternoon the blue clouds hid the sea, but the sunlight dappled
the plains with an orange glow. The Rhône was a shining silver vapor,
and as far as the eye could see there were only the glowing plains and
the purple shadows: softness and ease far below, and the hard rock
underfoot. I knew now why the lords of Les Baux conquered southern France and why the Princess Alix battled for half a lifetime to
regain her inheritance. The rock commanded it.

SAINT-REMY-EN-PROVENCE

I lingered for a while on the heights of Les Baux, hoping the sky would clear completely, for I cannot imagine a better vantage point for looking over Provence. There was mist in the air and droves of blue-bellied clouds were throwing their purple shadows over the salt meadows, and the sea was no more than a rare quickening of light in the south. The wind roared against the rock and the starlings continued to chatter and fling themselves madly from one side of the cliff to the other, while I hoped the sky would suddenly grow bright again or the rain would fall, turning the great plains into lakes.

The blue-bellied clouds came lumbering along interminably, the winds grew cooler, and the chatter of the starlings never ended, while I waited for the sun to shine on the darkening plains. Soon it became cold, and there was nothing to be done except to wander back through the dusty confusion of ruins, the quarries and hollow tombs, of a place which was once rich in palaces. It was beyond belief that people once lived here. This rock has a distant resemblance to the Acropolis, and it is easy enough to imagine the processions making their way up the steep stairway to the Parthenon, for enough of the temple remains and we know the faces of the people. But of the faces and manners of the predatory lords of Les Baux we know almost nothing at all, and sometimes they seem older than the Athenians.

I drove down to Saint-Rémy along a winding road, haunted by

that emptiness, those broken walls and gulleys and honeycombs where everything was so ruined and decayed that it seemed to be dissolving into the living rock. A castle, a fortress, a donjon, graves cut into the stone shelves, all vanishing, and only the *columbarium*, a fretted stone beehive where funeral urns were once kept, standing up against the desolation of dust and ruins. The proud names and the tremendous titles echoed in the empty air—Princes of Orange, Kings of Arles, Emperors of Constantinople—and I thought of all the long-vanished empires which have left no arts by which they were remembered, and of how our own civilization seems to be working toward the same fate which overcame Les Baux.

But from Les Baux onward it is downhill all the way to the flowering valley thick with olive trees and wheatfields, and the neat villas which cannot have changed at all since Roman times. The taste of death hung over the dead city on the rock, but Saint-Rémy is overflowing with life, a small town, hardly more than a village, with painted windows and flower boxes and fountains in the squares. It is one of those towns where men carry their children on their shoulders, and there is a quivering gaiety below the calm surface.

Not very many people go to Saint-Rémy, and this is a pity, for there are few places so richly blessed. There are at least six reasons for going there. There is first the charm of the town itself, which seems to have withdrawn only a little from the traffic of the world, and then there are the two superb Roman monuments, one an archway and the other the mausoleum shaped like a jewel box, of which we have already spoken, and then there is the Greek city of Glanon with its rows of columns and glaring white roads, and then there is the small museum in the town, a model for all provincial museums because it is so clean and airy and well arranged. Finally there is the twelfth-century church with its delicate cloisters and the house where Vincent Van Gogh lived during a year of calm despair and madness.

In so small a town it is almost more than one can hope for—the concentration of so much energy within a little space. The white city of Glanon, the Roman monuments, the beautiful twelfth-century cloister and Van Gogh's madhouse are all within a stone's throw of one another. It is as though, quite deliberately, in the space of a few yards someone had deliberately designed an epitome of the arts of France, setting them against the improbable purple hills.

To come to this place in the afternoon, when the shadows lie heavy on the earth, is to enter a fairy tale. It is all familiar ground, for we know it well from Van Gogh's paintings. Indeed he set up his easel and painted in the cornfields which Henri Rolland has lovingly and patiently excavated; there was a buried city with marble columns ten feet below his paintbrush. Here he painted *The Reaper*, making many versions of a ghostly figure moving among the too-bright corn, the sky trembling on the tips of the flaring mountains. Behind him in a sunken field were the Roman monuments shining with a blue light, and to his left stood the church and the cloisters surrounded by cypresses, hallowed acres. Standing in that small sunken field with its triumphal archway and mausoleum dedicated to the grandsons of Caesar, looking toward the white city and then toward the cloisters, you have the feeling that you have come to the end of the journey. In that quietness, that serenity formed by the sloping landscape, there is a perfection I have found nowhere else in France. No wonder the poet Mistral called the small sunken field "the very heart of Provence."

THE BIRD DROPPINGS

There are not many places left which can be associated with Van Gogh. His house in Arles was bombed during the last war, and though the Night Café remains near the railroad station, and is dimly recognizable even now, there is only one remaining house in the south of France which can be associated with him directly, and this house is already falling into ruins. Here, at the bottom of the garden, he lived from May 1889 to May 1890, fighting off those attacks of madness which came with increasing frequency. He was ill and tired, and his voice was strangely hoarse, for when the attacks came he would shout at the top of his lungs hour after hour. There followed days and weeks of extraordinary lucidity in which he painted strenuously and as brilliantly as ever, sometimes locking himself up in a room and working slowly from morning to night. Sometimes, too, when he was calm, Dr. Peyron would let him go out into the fields and he would set up his easel facing the tormented blue crags of the Alpilles, painting the reapers and the wheatfields and the olive trees with their pale flowers, while swarms of midges and blue flies and emerald-rose beetles hovered over them like clouds of incense.

I walked along the pathway which leads to the church of Saint-Pierre-le-Mausolée, and there was not a vista which Van Gogh had not made peculiarly his own. One cannot see it except through his eyes, so completely has he conquered the land. This clump of hyacinth, those trees leaning in the wind, the spiraling cypresses, they all belong to him as though he had created them, as though they had sprung from his imagination. I used to think the gnarled and twisted hills in the background of his Saint-Rémy paintings were the product of a disordered mind, but in fact the hills are even sharper and more menacing than he painted them. The cypresses here leap like black flames, and so he painted them filled with an urgent, towering life. His colors have not changed, and all the landscapes belong to him.

It is the same with the cloister, which he painted several times: it is a very primitive cloister with none of the magnificence of Saint Trophime and Moissac, very quiet and humble. The capitals are decorated with birds, seashells, leaves, sun wheels and tentative little animals which peer out shyly among the stone leaves as though they were not quite certain what they are doing there. The Mother Superior was walking in the cloister, enormous, black-gowned, pink-faced, with spectacles on the end of her nose. I asked her whether I could see the rooms where Van Gogh lived in the yellow stone building at the bottom of the garden.

She flung up her hands in horror, and there was a great stirring of keys and chains and rosaries.

"No one can go there," she said. "Not at all possible—no one can go."

"I only want to go for a few minutes—"

"And break your head, young man! Goodness, how foolhardy people are!"

It was all a mystery. She kept flinging up her hands, smiling with

conscious superiority over the young who were continually disturbing her meditations with requests to visit this place. Did they not
know it was forbidden? Was it sensible to jeopardize the lives of so
many good people? And this Van Gogh, this painter, this man who
was ill in soul and body, and who never showed the slightest con-
trition for his evil ways—she had heard that he lived among prostitutes
and had even presented one of them with a portion of his ear—surely
this man was not worth bothering about! That very morning some
Germans had come and tried to bribe her, in order to see the rooms,
and she had quite properly sent them packing.

So I said rather hopelessly: "Nevertheless, *ma mère*, he is regarded
by many as the saint of our time."

"Who says so?" she flared, and once more she threw out her hands
and there was a jingle of keys and rosaries and slender silver chains.

"Did he belong to the true faith?"

"No, *ma mère*, but he was a Christian, a very good Christian, and
he truly sacrificed himself for others."

She was in a temper now, and I knew it was nearly impossible to
shake her. Red spots were appearing on her pink cheeks, and we
seemed to be going faster and faster round the cloister, and the noise
of the keys and rosaries was growing louder. At last she stopped dead
on her tracks, and a curious tight-lipped smile appeared on her thin
lips.

"No, you can't go there," she said. "The wooden beams are all
worn, and it's more than your life is worth to go there. If there's an
accident, what will people say of us?"

I said I would cheerfully risk an accident, but she shook her head
sharply. She had made up her mind. All my arguments had only assured her that she had been right from the beginning. She was an
imperious woman, and I imagine she ruled over the nuns with a hand
of iron.

"No," she said, and she looked like an empress at that moment,
though her spectacles were slipping off the end of her nose. "No, it
is not possible. Later, perhaps, when the floors have been repaired it
may be possible. There can be no argument. I have made up my
mind."

I wondered why she had spent so long making up her mind, but there was nothing to be done. I went outside and spoke to the gate-keeper, a little birdlike woman dressed in black who must have been nearly eighty.

"I told you you wouldn't be able to see those rooms," she chirruped. "Didn't I tell you?"

"You did."

"She doesn't let anyone see the rooms. Only if you have a gun, *monsieur*—"

"What do you mean—a gun?"

"Like I told you—if you aim a gun at the Mother Superior, she will let you see the rooms."

"I wouldn't think of aiming a gun at her."

"Not you, *monsieur*, but during the war a German general came here. He, too, wanted to see the room where the painter died. The Mother Superior refused, but he pulled a gun on her, and of course the Mother Superior is a sensible woman and she took him to the rooms—only they were not the rooms of the painter. The general wore a black uniform, and there was a skull and crossbones on his cap. He had a big revolver, and he said *poum-poum*, and the Mother Superior went as white as a sheet. You see, *monsieur*, it is quite impossible to see the room where he died."

I am not sure that I believe the story. I have a feeling that the Mother Superior was impervious to the threats of S.S. generals.

"He didn't die here," I said. "He died at Auvers a few weeks after he left Saint-Rémy."

"No, he died here, *monsieur*."

"All right, he died here. Where did he die?"

"In the large room overlooking the wheatfield. You cannot miss the room. There are bars over the windows. It hasn't changed very much, they say, except the floors are rotting away. You can see it quite plainly if you walk along the wall—"

So in the gathering dusk I wandered along the wall and stood below the window of the yellow house, and there was nothing to see except the green shutters and a broken pane of glass, and somehow it was enough. The window looked over a plowed field and a row

Venus of Toulouse

Le Puy

Carcassonne

Aigues-Mortes

Abbey Church of Saint Denis

Chartres Cathedral

The Treasures
of Saint Denis

Montségur

of cypresses. The room had a northern light, and was quite large. For hour after hour Van Gogh stood by the window, puffing at his pipe and sometimes sipping a glass of wine. "A pipe, a glass of wine, some bread and cheese and the works of Shakespeare, these are the remedies which the incomparable Dickens prescribed against suicide," he wrote to his brother Theo, and he found in Shakespeare the same qualities he found in Rembrandt. "Rembrandt," he wrote, "has a tenderness of gaze, a heart-broken tenderness, a glimpse of super-human infinitude—and in many places Shakespeare has them too."

In that room he read *King Lear* and was so overwhelmed that he rushed out into the garden and looked closely at the blades of grass, an ear of wheat, the branch of a fir tree: for these, being quiet and untormented, had power to heal. A few days later he wrote to his sister in Holland that he had been painting an old withered, sunburned woman, pock-marked and ugly, "as insignificant as a blade of grass," and this woman too had power to heal his wounds. Yet, for a whole year, he rarely left his room. What he feared above all was an attack in the open air, when he was beyond human help. At such times he was overwhelmed with a sense of shattering loneliness and he had the strange delusion that "people were coming towards me from a great distance, greatly changed and unrecognizable." Once he had said he would grow strong amid storms—"*Je grandirai dans la tempête.*" But it was this strange disease, this storm within himself, which finally destroyed him. He left Saint-Rémy in May, and one afternoon in July at Auvers-sur-Seine, near Paris, he shot himself in the groin when he was out in the fields, and crawled back to the inn to die. In all his life he had never sold a painting.

Today it is almost beyond belief that things could have happened in this way. It is as though he invented a vocabulary, and we speak his language, whether we like it or not. We cannot look at a wheat-field, sunflower or a cypress tree except through his eyes, and all of southern France belongs to him. From Saint-Rémy to Les Saintes Maries every landscape seems to bear in red paint in a corner the indelible signature of VINCENT.

What is puzzling is that there could ever have been a time when his fame was not assured. Van Gogh himself never doubted his eventual fame; he seems to have known very early in his career that he possessed a life-giving power that would bridge the centuries, and with every passing year he was more certain of it. His contemporaries, seeing those crusts of hard paint on the canvas, quietly consigned him to oblivion.

The gatekeeper, the little birdlike woman dressed in black, was waiting for me when I returned from the plowed field and an oblique look at Van Gogh's studio. Because she was very old, and must have known people who had known Van Gogh, I asked her whether she could remember any stories about him.

She thought for a while, and then she said: "I remember the Mother Superior—not the present one, but the one before her—saying she had seen him painting. She said it was the painting of the devil."

"Is that all she said?"

"She said it was an offense against God. She said he didn't know anything about painting. It was just like covering the canvas with the droppings of birds—*le kaka des oiseaux!*"

Saying this, she smiled her bright smile and then vanished behind the heavy gates, while I wandered away past the delicate jewel box erected to the grandsons of Caesar down the long road to Saint-Rémy.

LE PUY

I think I could wander forever in the south of France, going from village to village and from church to church, but in the end I find myself always returning to the towns where my ancestors sprang from. My roots are in Provence and the Auvergne and along the banks of the Rhône, in towns so ancient that no one knows their beginnings: Greeks, Gauls and Romans were in all of them. These towns are Aix-en-Provence, Vienne and Le Puy, and for me they are the most beautiful places in France. One town ruled a kingdom, another a province of the Roman Empire, and the third was a place of pilgrimage. Now all these places lie in the quiet backwaters, far from the main stream of power.

In the Middle Ages people came from all over France to worship in Le Puy and to make offerings to the Black Virgin in the cathedral. I suspect that even before the coming of Christianity people flocked to worship in the city, for there is something very mysterious about the place which would attract worshipers. Hundreds of thousands of years ago a volcano erupted, spitting out lava which hardened in weird and formidable shapes; and the town lies clustered at the foot of the lava slopes. On one of these dark towering cones stands the cathedral, on another there is a statue of the Virgin made from two hundred guns captured at the battle of Sevastopol, and on the third, the most precipitous of all, stands a small and beautiful Romanesque chapel in honor of Saint Michel d'Aiguilhe—Saint Michael of the Needle, the high pointed place, close to the sky. Those sudden mountains have something of the effect of the gnarled rocks placed deliberately, but with such apparent casualness, in a Japanese garden. It is as though some very mysterious meaning had been attached to them, as though they were appointed for some purpose known only to the wise. But these mountains have many moods, and on a bright sunny day the landscape appears to be leaping with exuberance.

Robert Louis Stevenson, who set off from Le Puy to write his *Travels with a Donkey in the Cévennes,* thought he had come to a Scottish landscape, and found the people dour and given over to violent political beliefs, though he added that their dourness seemed to vanish on acquaintance and their political beliefs were no more turbulent than most. For myself, I always found them gentle to excess, without cunning, and curiously remote from the people of central France and of Provence, living on the frontierlands, strangely content in their isolation. During the savage winters when the mountain passes are deep in snow they turn inward and look into themselves, living on their dreams. Perhaps it was for this reason that so many of them became Crusaders and mercenaries adventuring in distant lands. The chronicles of the Crusades are full of their exploits, and Lafayette, who was born near Le Puy, followed in their footsteps.

Even today the life of Le Puy revolves around the cathedral, a superb Romanesque church housing the Black Virgin, which originally—for it was lost during the Revolution and another has replaced it—was a gift from Saint Louis on his return from the Holy Land. Saint Louis was only one of many French kings who came here on pilgrimage: altogether fourteen kings came to kneel before the high altar and to offer the vast treasure which was the pride of the Church in the Middle Ages. Today there is only a little treasure left—a piece of the True Cross, a Thorn, and one of the Virgin's slippers. The most valuable treasure is the Bible of Theodulphus, written on vellum in a beautiful Carolingian script in the eighth century, with gold initials on purple vellum. It is the most sumptuous book I have ever seen.

The Black Virgins were the fountains of blessing in the Middle Ages, but their history goes back to prehistoric times. They were rudely carved, and if they had been carved otherwise some of the power would have gone from them. Today not many survive: but the little black wooden figure arrayed in sumptuous robes still has power to move the soul as she stands in that vast and eerie cathedral with its red-and-white arches like those at Cordova. Saracenic influence lies heavy on the cathedral, and there is even a wooden doorway with inscriptions in Kufic letters. Did Arab workmen help to build the Cathedral? No one seems to know.

Like the Bible of Theodulphus, the cathedral has a sumptuous air, but for the purest Romanesque you must climb the two hundred and fifty steep stairs to Saint Michel d'Aiguilhe, which was built by Bishop Gottschalk in 962. Once it was a small hermitage called Séguret, the place of safety, where a man could be alone with his God. Now it is known chiefly for the exquisite carving on the twelfth-century portal, where the Lamb is worshiped by the blessed, while two charming mermaids lie in wait for the unwary. The same theme is represented in Moissac with almost terrifying power and grandeur. Here there is no terror nor any grandeur: only a quiet joy. Instead of God in Majesty there is a gentle Lamb; instead of lions there are mermaids. On the capitals eagles and human faces emerge from garlands of leaves.

The portal of Saint Michel d'Aiguilhe has the charm which comes from certainty, with no straining for effect. It seems not to have been made, but to have grown out of the living rock, very quietly and insistently. Inside the small chapel there are the faint splashes of red and blue paint, the traces of twelfth-century frescoes, and if you look closely you can distinguish an entry into Jerusalem and a flaming Archangel at war with an invisible dragon.

Le Puy lies below, red-roofed and quiet in the cup of the hills. Here the air is clear, with the sweet taste of the mountain springs. Sometimes, mysteriously, a wraith of mist will form in the valley on clear summer days. At such times, standing by that delicately carved portal, you find yourself envying the monks who once climbed up the living rock to the hermitage and never returned.

THE LACE MAKERS

When I lived as a boy in Le Puy, there were two men who absorbed my affections. One was my uncle, Auguste Bérard, a manufacturer of lace, and the other was the local pharmacist, whom we called Monsieur Chossegros, because it was inconceivable that he was ever young or ever possessed a Christian name. My uncle was lean and tall, with twinkling blue eyes and a ruddy face and a white military mustache which, as I remember it, grew smaller and smaller as the years passed, until it almost vanished in the benevolence of his smile. My uncle had square shoulders and his whole appearance was faintly military, but this came, I think, from his incessant wanderings over the mountains of the Auvergne during his younger days when he marched from village to village collecting lace and giving new patterns to the villagers. On these journeys he carried large sums of money, and because he was always alone he carried a stout cudgel.

I doubt whether Monsieur Chossegros ever carried a cudgel, or ever walked more than half a mile from his shop. In appearance he was the opposite of my uncle. He was monstrously, absurdly fat; he had a pale, round, blubbery face which he disguised with an enormous walrus mustache; and he waddled and wobbled in immense black boots which made a flapping sound on the pavement. He wore a flowing cravat and smelled of the pharmacy; and while my uncle had the sweetest smile I have ever known in a man, Monsieur Chossegros was incapable of anything so simple as a smile. At the least provocation he would burst out into peals of high-pitched, crackling laughter. There would be, first, a kind of subdued shaking, a preliminary unsettling of the blubber, followed by a queer, inarticulate rending sound from somewhere in the depths of his throat, and this would be followed by wheezings and coruscations of noise rising up the windpipe, and at last there would come that fearful, whinnying explosion of laughter which always fascinated and terrified me because it lasted so long and reduced him to such imbecile helplessness. His confusion was pitiable. He would mop his brow, weave his body into all kinds of positions in the hope of relieving these terrible fits of laughter by a change of posture, and then gradually, by exerting all his will power, he would take command, inch by inch, of that mountain of blubber which threatened to burst through his clothes.

My uncle and Monsieur Chossegros were inseparable companions. Every night for thirty years they had gone to the same café on the Place de Breuil and played the same game of cards in the evening. For thirty years they had exchanged remarks about the weather, about politics and about the leading figures of the small town, and there must have come, I suppose, a period when there was nothing of importance left to say to one another, when their friendship continued only by courtesy of habit. Yet this was not at all the appearance they gave. They hugely enjoyed each other's company, and never stopped speaking to each other. There was, like a chorus to all the days I spent in Le Puy, the grave, beautifully modulated voice of my uncle interrupted by the continual squeaks and firecracker explosions of Monsieur Chossegros.

I never learned how or why they became so intimate, and I suspect there was a distant family connection. Certainly the lace maker had little need of the professional services of the pharmacist, and the pharmacist had little need of lace. Probably what held them together was a certain philosophy which they held in common, a philosophy which is difficult to describe without seeming sententious, because it involves an almost miraculous patience and generosity. I remember going into Monsieur Chossegros's pharmacy, and when the loud ringing of the doorbell had given place to the proprietor's squeaks, growls and rumblings, there was a long pause followed by an all-embracing sweeping of the arms. "So you've come?" he said. "Is there anything you want—anything at all? Would you like this green frog? How about peppermints? Let's sit down and find out what you really want." The same technique was followed by my uncle. There was a whistle pipe leading from the dining room on the first floor to the shop on the ground floor. From the dining room you had only to blow down the pipe to attract the attention of the people in the shop, and you could then carry on talking through the pipe. Voices up and down the pipe were strangely muffled. I enjoyed blowing down the pipe at all hours of the day, and my uncle always answered.

Any other man would have been driven silly. Once when I was ten or eleven he drew me aside and said with perfectly grave face: "I've been thinking about the most beautiful things in life. Oh, they are not at all what you think. The best thing of all is when you bite into a good round red apple." Then he emptied his pocket of apples, and we enjoyed life together.

In those days my uncle was perhaps the richest man in Le Puy, for lace was booming. In the early 1920's everyone wanted lace. Curtains were made of lace, and so were dresses and handkerchiefs and tablecloths and church vestments and women's undergarments. In the villages around Le Puy a hundred thousand people were making lace for export, chiefly to England, Germany and America. I would go to the villages and hear the clicking of the bobbins long before I reached the first house; and there would be women of all ages sitting in the sun outside their houses, wearing little lace caps, their nimble hands moving with marvelous dexterity as they manipulated the bobbins on their laps. But already the machines were coming in. In the old days my uncle spent his time wandering through the hills, but now he had men to do his wandering for him, and he had an automobile to take him to his factories, which were springing up all over the town. Though rich, he continued to live quietly over the shop and he continued to spend his evenings playing cards with Monsieur Chossegros. The last time I saw him he took me by the arm, smiled his breathtakingly sweet smile, and said: "Apples are the most marvelous thing in the world, aren't they?"

I never saw my uncle again, and more than thirty years passed before I went back to Le Puy. Much had changed. There were no more lace-capped women sitting in the sun outside the village doors. The lace factories no longer produced lace: they produced instead the queer meshes which women sometimes put in their hair to make it pile up. The days with single orders for ten thousand dollars' worth of lace had gone forever. Yet there seemed to be no poverty in the town. Life went on quietly and vigorously, and the air was still bracing, and Saint Michel d'Aiguilhe was as beautiful as ever. A resistance fighter had been killed by the Germans just outside the house where I had spent so much of my boyhood, and there was a plaque on the wall celebrating his heroism. There were hurdy-gurdies and Coca-Cola stands in the great square looking out over the park, and the pharmacy near the statue of Lafayette was still in business.

"Do you remember Monsieur Chossegros?" my cousin Henri asked me.

"Of course I do!"

"He's dead now. He died nearly thirty years ago. But I was passing it yesterday and saw something I thought would interest you. Come and look!"

So we passed the pharmacy, and there very faintly on the glass door could be seen the shapes of the enamel letters, long removed, which proclaimed him to be the owner of the shop. In this ghostly fashion he had survived—a mountain of a man, and the happiest I ever knew.

ROUEN

That day the clouds were of an astonishing whiteness, racing furiously across the heavens, and there was snow in the air. I remember it was near the New Year and the children all muffled up like bears were crowding the streets and peering into the shop windows for the toys they would soon be receiving, for New Year's Day is a greater feast than Christmas in France. Rouen is not the most inviting place in winter. The cold winds come over the Normandy plains, whistling through the narrow streets. Much of the town was bombed to smithereens, and the new buildings have a raw, unimpressive smoothness, and the damp clings to the improbable walls of the few remaining medieval houses. The great churches—and Rouen has more than enough of them—are like hollowed-out icebergs in winter. On the cold station platform and in the icy streets I wondered what I was doing in Rouen on a winter's day.

There was so much excitement in the streets that I thought I had come on the feast day of the patron saint of the city or a mass distribution of rosettes of the Legion of Honor, but it was two days before the New Year and a market day with all the villagers from miles around bringing their produce to sell in the squares. So there were great heaps of flowers, vegetables and quartered lambs and disemboweled oxen, the fresh blood gleaming in that frosty air like garnets and rubies, and more and more carts kept coming in from the country, impeding the traffic in the narrow streets with their bulging sides of beef, and the blood dripped on the cobblestones. It was pleasant to listen to the clomp and clatter of the horses' hooves and the shrieking and groaning of the drivers of Simcas who could make no headway. The countryfolk were pouring into the town, and by afternoon they were in full possession.

The strange thing is that Rouen has not changed more over the centuries. In spite of the bombings and the new factories and the seagoing ships on the Seine, it still wears its medieval air, and the builders of the cathedrals would find themselves in familiar territory if they returned. They would be lost in the port area, but in the center of the city there would be enough landmarks to light their way. Coming out of the railroad station, they would recognize the Tour Jeanne d'Arc, that massive fortress tower which is all that remains of a six-towered castle built by King Philip Augustus in 1205 after he had won Normandy from King John of England, and having inspected the tower they would go on to the churches and the gateways and the market squares, where they would see faces which have not changed over the centuries: the rosy-cheeked, fair-haired, heavy-boned Normans still look more like Englishmen than Frenchmen. It was from Rouen that William set out for the conquest of England, and that tall, heavy-boned, immensely corpulent man with a red face and a high, bald forehead, walking in spite of his corpulence with an immense and savage dignity—so William of Malmesbury describes him—cannot have looked very different from those farmers in the market place, thickset and florid, quick to violence and shouting themselves hoarse.

William was Duke of Rouen before he became conqueror of England. A comet flamed across the sky of Europe in the year of his conquest, and violence was his companion all his life. Once when a besieged city hung tanners' hides on its walls to mock him, he cut off the hands and feet of his prisoners and tore out their eyes, and hurled them across the battlements. He destroyed everything that stood in his path, left England a desert, and made the king of France miserable with his border raids. The story is told that he was lying ill in Rouen when he heard that King Philip was jesting about the candles which would be offered in church to celebrate his recovery. William swore the strongest oath he knew—*"Per resurrectionem et splendorem Dei!"*—"By the Resurrection and the splendor of God I shall have a hundred thousand candles burning, and all of them at Philip's expense!" When he was well again he set out to capture Mantes, and he put the city to the flames. He was riding over the hot embers of the burning city when his horse stumbled and he was wounded by the high iron pommel of his saddle. He was carried back to Rouen, where he died in agony a few weeks later, and his body was floated down the Seine for burial in Caen. As the funeral procession made its way through Caen, the streets, according to the ancient chronicler, burst into flame. It was a fitting end for a conqueror.

JOAN OF ARC

When Joan of Arc was led through the streets of Rouen to be burned at the stake, she too was a conqueror. She had led armies into battle and suffered wounds and put a king on a throne, and heard the voices of the saints and debated with the most learned theologians of her time, and all this before she was nineteen. No one like her had ever appeared in France before, and none ever appeared again.

Today in the Vieux Marché you can still feel the presence of Joan of Arc, though it is no more than a ghostly breath. The whole market place has changed, and there is not one building which was standing in her time. The old church of Saint Sauveur has gone, pulled down by the revolutionaries in 1794, and all the rows of squat houses which appear on Jacques Le Lieur's famous map have perished long ago. Yet the square is still a market place, roughly the same size as in the days when she was being tried, tawdry as all such squares must be, noisy and evil smelling, and yet with a kind of commonplace grandeur about it. The haggling goes on, and there is always the sense of being at the beating heart of the city. There are good restaurants on the square, and a terrible waxwork show where, having penetrated through the black curtains, you come upon Joan in armor, and you are surprised to find she has the face of some waxwork from a milliner's window.

From paintings and drawings made shortly after her death we have a fair idea of her appearance. She had one of those rather full and singularly calm faces which can still be seen among the peasants of Lorraine, with a high forehead and a delicate chin. Her hair was dark and fell neatly down her back. Her eyes were enormous, and her hands were long and thin. In her appearance and in her manner there was a quiet authority, a quiet exaltation.

But on the day when she was led out to die in the Vieux Marché between a fountain and a churchyard, she was a pitifully broken woman. The voices had told her she would be saved by a great victory; the angels would descend and carry her away in their arms; but there were no angels. There was only the raw morning light and the soldiers milling about in the streets.

She was led out of the prison and made to stand in a cart, wearing the gray frock of a penitent, and a cap of the same material. She was not bound, for there was no possibility of escape: eighty soldiers marched beside the cart. Small and frail, barefoot, holding to the sides of the cart for support, she was led through the winding streets, and sometimes she would make little despairing gestures as though she hoped for a word of sympathy, but all the onlookers were frozen into silence.

Her beauty remained, but she looked much older than her nineteen years, her face very thin, with dark rings under her eyes, for she had slept little during the preceding weeks and less during the past few days, because the jailors had been attempting to rape her. Every window was crowded, and there were even people clinging to the roofs. All the way to the Vieux Marché Joan was weeping bitterly, and the sunlight caught the wetness on her cheeks, turning them silver. Her execution had been ordered for eight o'clock in the morning, but it was nearly nine o'clock when the cart entered the square, which she had never seen before. All her rare journeys through Rouen had taken place in another part of the town altogether.

The square in those days was flanked by the church of Saint Sauveur, a meat market, and two rows of houses. Facing the church was a scaffold about eight feet high, made of brick, of a very practical construction, for there were air vents leading through the roof of the scaffold, which resembled a small circular house. The pillar was made of stone, and was well anchored. That morning, together with an enormous quantity of firewood, barrels of tar and tubs of oil lay at the foot of the scaffold, which was black with the flames of previous burnings.

Feverishly, during the night, a large number of platforms had been erected all round the Vieux Marché for the guests who would attend the complex ceremonies of execution, for the killing of a condemned prisoner is never simple. The punishment must be deliberately prolonged; every last ounce of guilt must be extracted from the prisoner, and if the prisoner is innocent, there is all the more reason why a complicated ritual must be carried out. The principal platforms were occupied by the bishops and the priests. The bishops had chosen to be seated on a platform overlooking the square in the grounds of the cemetery of the church of Saint Sauveur, while the priests chose to sit with their backs to the meat market. Around the strange, ugly, black scaffold was a ring of English soldiers. The English were the occupying power in Rouen, under the command of the Duke of Bedford, English regent of France and brother of Henry V, and he too was present in the square, standing on another platform; and these different platforms, and all the others on which the townspeople were congregated, spoke of the division of responsibility among all those who watched her die. Everyone could claim afterward that he had only a small share in her death.

The cart stopped where the priests were assembled, and here Joan was compelled to listen to a brief sermon on her sins and the fate reserved for her in Hell. She listened attentively, and when it was over she called on the priests to pray for her soul and to say Masses for her. Her strength was returning. She was no longer weeping as she asked pardon of her judges and her executioners, but the priests wept, and even Cauchon, who was about to pronounce her death sentence, or rather to hand her over to the secular arm, could be seen weeping. And now the cart moved a little way to the place where the bishop sat, and one of his serving men climbed into the cart and removed her gray cap and put in its place a curious pasteboard cap like a bishop's mitre, wider at the top than at the bottom, on which someone had written the words: *Heretic, Relapsed Sinner, Apostate, Idolater*. These words were written round the wider portion of the cap, while underneath there were painted devils representing Belial, Satan and Behemoth; and no doubt this was done in a kind of imitation of her own banner, which showed a small painting of Christ attended by two angels, with the words IHS MARIA. When her own cap was removed, it was seen that her head was shaven, and this too was part of her punishment.

Cauchon read the verdict, pronouncing her a corrupt member who must be severed from the Church, and utterly abandoned by the Church for the harm she had done. She was then officially excommunicated, and this solemn recital of the deed of excommunication disturbed her more than anything else that had happened that morning, for she fell to her knees and sobbed helplessly, alone in the cart.

She was then given over to the English, who hated her for having led the French on so many battlefields, and they were moreover inclined to regard her as a witch rather than as a heretic and apostate. The eighty soldiers accompanied the cart to the scaffold, and she was helped down. The great heap of fagots already lay on the scaffold, ready for the burning. On a wooden board nailed to the stake someone had written out a rather longer list of her crimes than appeared on her pasteboard hat. It read: "Jehanne, who has caused herself to be called the Maid, a liar, pernicious deceiver of people, soothsayer, blasphemer, idolatress, invoker of devils, apostate, heretic. . . ." All this was written in French, but it was not a very large board and very few people can have seen it from the platforms arranged round the square.

Standing at the foot of the scaffold, before she had been lifted up, she said: "Am I not to be given a cross?"

An English archer made a rough cross for her from the fagots, while she was being lifted up to the scaffold, and her hands still being free she was able to take it when the archer passed it up to her at the end of a stick. She kissed the cross, which was very small, and tucked it into the neck of her frock to lie against her breast. Then she called down to her confessor, Isambard de la Pierre, asking for another cross to be held before her eyes while she was dying, and he ran into the church of Saint Sauveur and returned in a few minutes with one of those long gilded crosses which are used in processions, and standing some distance from the scaffold he raised it so that she could see it. She did not take her eyes from the cross until she was dead.

Raoul le Bouteiller, the bailiff of Rouen, was now in charge of the ceremonies, and it was his task, as chief magistrate, to sentence her to death. But everything that morning had happened with the strange inevitability of nightmares and nothing happened according to rule. He did not sentence her to death. He simply told the executioner: "Do your duty," and retired to a safe distance.

Meanwhile the executioner, masked according to the custom of the age, was binding her to the stone pillar which rose in the middle of the scaffold. Her hands were pulled back behind the pillar and the wrists were roped together, and there were more cords round her neck, her waist, her legs and her ankles. She was now weeping uncontrollably. Someone heard her crying: "Rouen, Rouen, shall I die here? Shall this be my resting place? Ah, Rouen, how afraid I am that you shall suffer for my death!" Then the fagots heaped all round her were lit in four places. She was not alone on the scaffold, for two Dominican priests, who had pity for her, had jumped onto the scaffold at the last moment to console her or hear her confession, and they were still standing there when the first flames rose; and the robe of one of the priests was scorched before he was able to jump down.

The executioner had considerable experience of burning heretics, and the fagots had been arranged in such a way as to prolong the agony. At first there was little smoke, only the crackling of the fagots in a ring round the edge of the scaffold. If there had been much smoke, she might have suffocated to death long before the burning. But while the wood crackled, she could be heard screaming in fear, and then she quieted a little, and those who were close to her say she called out the names of the saints and the archangels, and she said "Jesus!" many times.

The crowd had swept into the square and surrounded the scaffold, but as the flames rose higher they were forced back by the heat. Only Isambard de la Pierre, and the two Dominicans, Martin Ladrenu

and Jean Massieu, remained close to her, and they were able to remember years later that she had distinctly called upon Saint Catherine
and Saint Marguerite, and had spoken the name of Jesus six times
before her whimpers turned into one last lingering scream, and then
it was all over.

With a long rake the executioner parted the fire to show her naked
and blackened body, with the head lolling on her breast. He knew
what was expected of him, that the body must be reduced to cinders
so that no one would ever be able to find a piece of her that could be
transformed into a holy relic. So Geoffoy Thieurache, the executioner, threw more fagots onto the scaffold, and later pitch and sul-
phur were added, and the flames rose again in a sickly, evil-smelling
conflagration, thick purple smoke filling the square, and people went
about choking and coughing. At last when the flames were quite low,
it was seen that her heart and entrails were not yet burned.

Henry Beaufort, bishop of Winchester, ordered her remains to be
thrown into the Seine, and this was done about six o'clock in the
evening.

As the bishop had hoped, no relics and almost nothing that once
belonged to her survived. Soon she was almost forgotten. The English remembered her, if they remembered her at all, as a witch who
was burned in the market place in the days when Rouen belonged to
them. The French were glad to be rid of her, and only a handful of
her friends remembered her. Twenty-five years after her death she
was solemnly rehabilitated, but this was a political act performed to
discredit the English and to add glory to the French crown. Her real
life—her life in the hearts of men—began long after her death.

In Rouen nothing that was touched by her remains except the
tower where she was imprisoned and the garden in the church of
Saint Ouen where she was once examined. There survive no coats of
mail, no swords, no letters written entirely in her hand. There are no
portraits done from life. Only one object belonging to her has survived, and this is a small, close-fitting helmet of the type called *bacinet
à visière* which hung for many years in her memory over the altar of
the church of Saint Pierre de Martroi at Orléans. The helmet has lost
its visor, but even without the visor it is a superb example of the

armorer's art, with great purity of line. Strangely it hides in an obscure corner of the collection of armor in the Metropolitan Museum in New York.

We do not know exactly where she died. The famous map of Rouen by Jacques Le Lieur, which shows the position of the scaffold, was not drawn until 1526, and is carelessly inked on parchment. The Rouennais are themselves not sure where the scaffold was. They have marked a red cross on the motor road going through the square, and she may have died there. Ten feet away on the sidewalk there is a smooth sheet of marble protected by an iron grille, and this is sometimes regarded as the place of martyrdom. Some fifteen feet from the slab of marble, against the back of the covered market, there is her statue, and some say she died where the statue is. If Jacques Le Lieur's map is correct, she must have died well inside the covered market among the red carcasses of beef, where the blood still drips noisily on the stone floors.

THE GARDEN HOUSE

The snow still hung in the air, and the churches shone with a ghostly whiteness. Those churches are superb, but the wind blows through them and they are bitterly cold in winter. Ruskin called the great cathedral "the most exquisite piece of pure Flamboyant work existing," and so it is, with its white tongues of broken flame leaping up the façade and its forest of flamelike pinnacles. I suspect the cathedral is best in winter, with the snow capping the pinnacles and sheeting the façade. But the interior was dark and damp, and I have no liking for ornate Renaissance tombs and escaped to the church of Saint Ouen, coldly austere and almost unornamented.

Saint Ouen has not the grace of Coutances, the loveliest of the Norman churches, but it has more quietness. They say that Saint Ouen was used as a blacksmith's shop during the Revolution, and the fine gray and faintly bluish color of the stone comes from the smoke of the blacksmith's fires. Coutances soars and exults and dazzles with a multitude of lights, and its proportions have a dangerous perfection. Saint Ouen is so vast that you are hardly aware of its proportions, and yet it is restful and self-assured, having no rose windows to disturb the gray-blue-silvery plainness of the interior. Some trick of optics enables you to see the reflection of the whole church is the holy water stoup; and there, muted, almost colorless, in enchanted miniature, are the curving gray pillars and the melting silvery windows. There come moments of weakness when you find yourself wondering whether Saint Ouen is not the greatest of French churches, because it is the most deeply mystical and religious, outshining even Chartres in its purity, which needs no embellishments.

In the streets the bustle of a winter market day was still going on. The farm carts lumbered by, the shops were full, the crowds were everywhere. Rouen with its twenty churches was always a materialist's paradise, given over to trade. Here in 1381 a mob seized the city, murdered the Abbot of Saint Ouen, who was its absolute ruler, and crowned a draper as their king. It seems to have been an act perfectly in keeping with the spirit of the city.

Later in the afternoon I drove out to Croisset, a few miles downstream from Rouen. Croisset has only one claim to fame—a single room overlooking the Seine, in the shadow of an enormous yellow paper factory. This room is Flaubert's garden house, where he liked to come on moonlight nights to gaze across the Seine, and sometimes he would throw a fishing line out the window in the stillness of a summer night. On such nights the little garden house was drowned in the smell of honeysuckle and roses.

The great white house where Flaubert spent the greater part of his life has gone; there remains only the garden house and a small garden with a flagstone path. Flaubert himself believed that this property once belonged to the monks of Saint Ouen, who used to divert themselves there in summer, and there is a pleasant legend that the Abbé Prévost wrote his scandalous novel *Manon Lescaut* within its walls. In those days Croisset was an unspoiled village far from Rouen. Now it is a suburb.

Today it takes an effort of the imagination to see the garden house as it was in Flaubert's time. The noise is deafening. Factories, warehouses, derricks, cranes are everywhere. The quiet towpath beside the river has become the main highway to Paris, crowded with ten-ton trucks, thick with gasoline fumes. Great coils of yellow smoke rise from the smokestacks of the paper factory; sea-going ships steam so close to the shore you can hear the rattle and clatter of machinery. A hundred years ago Flaubert loved the place for its quietness, and when he went wandering in distant places he would dream of it with a sense of overwhelming affection. It was his refuge from the world, his retreat, the place where he could give himself up to dreams.

In those days he lived in the long white house overlooking the river, which his father, a surgeon, had bought in 1804. There was a wooded hill behind the house and a lawn leading down to a small jetty, rose gardens and a lime-tree walk and a farmhouse and some cows which supplied milk to the small family. The white house was not unlike many other country houses along the river bank owned by the rich merchants of Rouen, who even then were trying to escape from the smoke of the city. There were vast rooms cluttered with *bric-à-brac,* and the servants went about stealthily for fear of disturbing Flaubert at his work. He had a small income, lived there royally, and seemed uncomfortable whenever he was far from the estate.

The house, of course, has vanished, giving way to the rumbling paper factory which spews yellow smoke over the sky. The little garden house remains, though the tiles are flaking away and there are cracks in the gray-paneled walls. For a few more years it will remain, and then the highway will be broadened, or a truck will smash into it, or it will simply die of old age and fall onto the road.

What is puzzling is how he ever got into his beloved garden house, for he was a tall, heavy-set, paunchy man, with the face of a choleric Viking, and he walked—on the rare occasions when he permitted himself to walk, for he hated exercise—with the rolling gait of a sailor. He towered over most of his friends, and he must have filled the room almost to bursting. And when the shelves were filled with books, and the sofa and table were brought in, there was hardly room to move in. Sometimes he came here to escape from his domineering mother, but more often he came for the pure pleasure of it. The garden house was his own, never to be entered by anyone else except at his orders. Here he wrote some of the best pages of *Madame Bovary,* and in the silence of the night he would bellow out in his great rough voice those sentences which seem to have been orchestrated for a full orchestra, so rich they are in music. People who heard him said it was like listening to grand opera, and they remembered that he always removed his cravat so that he could give full vent to the famous "*gueuloir de Flaubert*." And if he performed well, if he was pleased with the great resounding phrases which poured from his lips, whether they were his own or another's, he would shout: "*Cochon!*"

He loved the white house and he loved the garden house, and he was always talking about them. In February, 1850, he was sailing down the Nile with his friend Maxime du Camp when he was suddenly overwhelmed by a surge of memories of his home. It was evening, the first day out of Cairo, and the pyramids were gliding past in the vermilion sunset, those white shapes against the sky reminding him of the white house he owned on the banks of the Seine. It was strange that the pyramids should have reminded him of the village of Croisset, but it was so. He saw the palm trees waving at the foot of the pyramids, and jotted down in his diary that they were "like nettles at the foot of the grave." He was in a somber mood, full of thoughts of death, which was perfectly proper in a romantic young man of twenty-nine. But a little while later, when it grew dark, his mood changed to a tender lyricism as he wrote in his thin spidery handwriting the gentlest of many evocations of his home:

Somewhere far away, on a more gentle and younger river,
I know a white house where the shutters are closed when I am away.
I know the poplars are stripped of their leaves, trembling in the cold
*   mists,*
And the ice floes are drifting downriver and being tossed on the frozen
*   shore.*
I know the cows are in their byres, and the espaliers are covered with
*   straw,*
And from the farmhouse chimney the white smoke rises into a gray
*   sky.*
I see the long Louis XVI terrace bordered with lime trees,
Where in summer I wander in my dressing gown.
Six weeks will pass, and then the trees will be budding,
And every little branch will be starred with scarlet.
Then come the primroses—green, yellow, rose iris—spreading all over
*   the lawn.*
O primroses, pretty ones, drop your seeds gently,
That I may see you in another spring!

I left the wall all tapestried with roses,
And a garden house on the edge of the river.
Honeysuckle climbs over the iron balcony.
At one o'clock of a July morning
It is good to fish there in the clear moonlight.

So he wrote with a sense of unappeasable longing in the darkness of an Egyptian night, but it was many months before he returned. He followed the Nile as far as Wadi Halfa on the edge of the Nubian Desert. Jerusalem, Baalbek, Rhodes and Athens followed; there were brief visits to Smyrna and Constantinople, where he sat at table with Madame Aupick, the wife of the French ambassador, who turned deathly pale when he mentioned his esteem for Baudelaire, for she was the poet's mother, and then it was Rome, where his own mother was waiting for him, stern and domineering as ever. Intoxicated with the East, which he never saw again, he returned to Croisset and set to work on *Madame Bovary*, chipping off the words from his breast bone at the rate of perhaps half a sentence a day.

No one ever worked so hard at writing as that red-faced Norman giant. He roared with anger over the intractability of words, and wrestled with them interminably: sometimes whole months passed before the second half of a sentence was completed to his satisfaction. At intervals he would fall into one of those strange nervous fits when the blood rushed to his head and all words were forgotten. At such moments, for some reason which no one has ever discovered, he saw everything brilliantly colored with a yellowish gold light. It was perhaps the East coming back to haunt him.

He was fifty-nine when he died at his work table on a beautiful spring day. He had spent the night working on the last chapters of a novel, and had risen late. Wearing his famous dressing gown, and puffing at a pipe, he was going through the morning mail when he was seized with a violent attack of apoplexy, and died. A year later the great white house overlooking the Seine was razed to the ground.

The little garden house survived by a miracle. In 1906 it was bought by public subscription. Pious hands have transformed it into a museum, decorating the walls with a pathetic collection of his possessions. Here are his pipe and tobacco jar, his quill pens, his reading board, his gold watch and his guns. There is his handkerchief, neatly folded, and, more ominously, the glass from which he swallowed just before death: there is a rumor that he drank poison from it. There is the death mask of his mother, and there is Jacques Callot's engraving of the Temptation of Saint Anthony. There is the stuffed green parrot which he borrowed from the Rouen Museum when he was writing *Un Coeur Simple:* the feathers are still glossy, and there is a faint touch of scarlet on the wings. There are a golden Buddha and a brass frog. Most surprising of all there is a small urn from Carthage containing the bones of a child burned and sacrificed to Moloch, sent to the museum in 1923 by an admirer of his novel *Salammbo.*

Today the gray air of half-mourning hangs over the garden house, which is almost too large for the accumulations of *bric-à-brac*, the faded daguerreotypes, the long-forgotten oleographs. Few people come here, and on the day I visited the museum I was told there had been no visitors for a month. A cold wintry light came through the uncurtained windows, and shone off the hard white marble floor. There was an air of desolation. The unending roar of traffic, and all the new factories and skyscrapers, have somehow sucked the life from the place. Yet all, or nearly all, that remains of Flaubert's earthly existence is contained within those gray walls, and it is worth a pilgrimage.

You see the place best from the garden, walking along the same pathways where Flaubert once walked. Toward dusk the heavy traffic on the road ceases for a while, and you can hear the birds again. At this hour the delicate proportions of the curved windows, pointed roof and exquisite wrought-iron balcony seem to stand out against the darkening sky, and it is not difficult to imagine Flaubert hurrying like a ghost from the great house, wrapped in a long white dressing gown, to keep his tryst with the moon.

It was nearly dark when I made my way back to Rouen, but there was enough light to see the letters painted on a warehouse in full view of the garden house: *Centre de réception de Bananes—Croisset.* How Flaubert would have hooted at that!

CHARLEVILLE

I spent the morning wandering over the battlefield at Sedan, under the gray clouds, with the wind whipping the trees, and hardly a person in sight. It was one of those mornings when one should be sitting at the fireside with a book, not wandering over muddy and forgotten battlefields.

Who remembers Sedan? There cannot now be anyone alive who fought in that curious war which the Emperor Napoleon III precipitated like a man bent on his own destruction. And if there are few who remember Sedan, there must be fewer who remember the little village of Balan, where the emperor had his headquarters and where in the cemetery he tried to kill himself and put an end to the Napoleonic dynasty. There, among the tombs, the emperor had fired a machine gun at the advancing Germans, hoping the machine gun would blow up in his face or that a chance shot from one of the German gunners hidden in the woods would kill him. It was there that he made the decision to surrender, and it was along that winding road which begins in a farmyard that he returned to Sedan and gave orders for the white flag to be flown.

For years I have been haunted by that scene—the aging emperor, who had smeared rouge over his pale cheeks so that his soldiers would not see his pallor, a sick man suffering from a bladder infection, barely able to ride a horse, wearing white gloves and smoking innumerable cigarettes—a man who looked less like an emperor than like a dying floor walker, and yet somehow, by some miracle of acquired dignity, he still retained the loyalty of his soldiers, who would break out into wild cheers of *"Vive l'Empereur!"* whenever he appeared among them, and hearing them he would smile uncomprehendingly. He was a man of sensibility with a quick intelligence and exquisite manners, and when he came to Balan he knew that the end was in sight—the end of imperial France, the end of the kings, the end of a thousand-year-old tradition. He was the successor of Charlemagne, and he was old and bent, and his hands were shaking, and sometimes his face would pucker up in a grimace of unbearable pain. Such a strange emperor to be wandering almost alone on a battlefield! From time to time people came up to him and asked questions and went away empty-handed, for he could give them nothing—the command of the armies had long ago been taken from him. The Prince of Moskowa suggested he should resume command, but the emperor merely nodded and gazed into the distance. A train with steam up was waiting for him in Sedan, but he refused to take refuge in flight, and in any case there was nowhere to hide. "I shall die with my soldiers," he said, but instead he died in exile, in bed, in a large country house in southern England. But his real death was at Balan, when he saw the Germans coming over the rise and he knew that nothing in the world could stop them. After him came the deluge.

I had been wandering for hours over the windswept hills, which have changed very little in the intervening years, though here and there a copse or a farmhouse indicated on the old maps has vanished. It is rolling country, thickly wooded, with the fields curving like immense green bubbles. The sky was a mass of tattered clouds racing toward Germany. It was about lunch time when I reached the cemetery. I had expected the usual terrible walled square with the mortuary chapel and the flowers made of painted tin, but it was completely unlike anything I had expected. It was a narrow oblong strip along the side of a hill immediately above a farmhouse: so small and lost and miserable a place that it seemed to have been placed there as an afterthought. The road to the cemetery was deep in mud and manure, and I wondered what I was doing there on a cold and blus-

tery afternoon until a farm boy emerged from the stables and, seeing
that I was a stranger, asked whether he could be of service.

He was a pleasant red-cheeked boy of about sixteen, and I told
him I wanted to find the place where Napoleon III had lifted a machine gun over the wall and fired at the Germans.

"Napoleon III?" he asked. "What was he doing here?"

"He had his headquarters here."

The boy's face fell.

"Where?"

"About twenty yards from where you are standing."

"I never heard of it," he said. "*J'ai jamais entendu parler de ça.*"

Soon the farmer who owned these fields appeared. He was a short
man with a heavy beard and a gruff way of speaking. Yes, he knew
that Napoleon III had passed through Balan. He had stayed in this
farm and left a silver cup as a souvenir—he had taken it out of his
saddlebag and given it to the former owner of the farm—had stayed
the night and left early in the morning. In fact Napoleon III had not
stayed the night at Balan, but there was nothing to be gained by
argument. What happened to the silver cup? The old farmer
shrugged. He remembered seeing it when he was young, but it had
vanished in the course of time. We were standing by the cemetery
wall when he suddenly leaned forward and said urgently: "In these
parts no one wants to think of Napoleon III—or the Germans either."

It was the same everywhere I went in Sedan, the old anger still
flaring, the sudden hatred in the voice, the horror welling out of
the past. Sedan still wears the scars of all its wars. The people are
quiet, sullen, frightened. They have heard the roaring of cannon so
often that it is as though they have grown accustomed to their fears.
I went to the small town library to find a map of the campaign of
1870. The librarian was a young man with an engaging smile, but he
looked glum when I made the request. "I doubt whether we have one
anywhere," he said, and at last produced a small tattered map in an
old book. He said: "We don't like to think of Napoleon III—or the
Germans either."

From Sedan it is only half an hour by train to Charleville, where
the poet Arthur Rimbaud was born. Rimbaud detested Charleville.

He called it "the most abysmally imbecile of all the little provincial towns." I wondered why, and still wonder, for there can be few provincial towns so beautiful. It has parks and tree-lined boulevards, a vast square, some exotic Renaissance houses, and one arm of the Meuse glides mysteriously at the foot of the town. The people are clear-eyed and walk quickly; they are handsome and well-dressed and the shops are full. Once Charleville was the capital of a small dukedom belonging to Charles Gonzaga, Prince of Mantua, who founded the town in 1610, having carved out a small principality for himself on the borders of France and Belgium. Prince Charles was a charming rake, a ferocious warrior, and he had the Mantuan love for beautiful buildings. The Place Ducale at Charleville is even more beautiful than the far more famous Place des Vosges in Paris. The red brick buildings are all exactly the same, with the same steep, sloping blue roofs; an arcade runs round the square and the statue of Prince Charles in feathered cap and knee boots quite properly occupies the center of the square. From the Place Ducale a short road leads down to the Old Mill which straddles the Meuse, but nothing could look less like a mill. It is of yellow brick, three stories high, ornamented with four enormous columns and the coat of arms of the ducal house of Mantua. Arthur Rimbaud lived in a small house facing the handsome mill.

For some reason I had expected a town of soot and smoke and belching chimneys. There would be narrow streets and gutters running with filth and old mildewed churches in disrepair. Instead, I found a town full of color and vitality, the girls in vivid print dresses, the fountains playing, the arcades full of bustling activity, the Meuse flowing sweetly beneath the tree-clad slopes of Mount Olympus on the other side of the river. The town was gay, like the coat of arms of Prince Charles, which consisted of a hand emerging from a white cloud and holding a sword which flowered into both a laurel wreath and a sunflower, and in the center of the sunflower two eyes, a nose and a mouth were delicately painted. This smiling sunflower, surmounted by a ducal crown, is still the coat of arms of the town.

I suspect that Rimbaud would have hated any provincial town, however beautiful. He would have detested the small, niggardly ways of the provinces, the lawyers and shopkeepers and poorly paid priests. He raged against the calm self-assurance of these small communities. "I am uprooted, sick, furious, a beast, confused," he wrote to his friend Georges Izambard when he was sixteen. "I had hoped for sun baths, infinite promenades, rest, voyages, adventures, bohemianism." He was to have more than enough of all these things in the years to come, but Charleville was curiously lacking in them. So he was always escaping from the town, and always coming back again.

He was star-crossed from the beginning. His father was a heavy-set handsome soldier from the south of France, a man who had fought in Algeria, Italy and the Crimea, who was made a Chevalier of the Legion of Honor in the year that Arthur was born. He was an intelligent man and a fine scholar, who translated the *Koran* into admirable French. His mother was a small, nervous, hysterical woman, a farmer's daughter, very close to the earth. She pinched pennies and there was no gaiety in her. Arthur, the second son, was born in October, 1854, and six years later Captain Frédéric Rimbaud marched out of the house, never to return. He was weary of his wife's nagging, and had no love for his two sons and three daughters.

Arthur was a precocious student at school, and his Latin verses written at the age of fourteen show him to be in full command of his style. In the following year he began to write verses in French, such a spate of them that modern commentators are only now beginning to put them in order. His sixteenth year was his *annus mirabilis*. Then he wrote poems which still have power to shock and dazzle us, and these poems are included in anthologies of French poetry. He was seventeen when he made the acquaintance of Verlaine, who left his wife to follow Arthur through England and Belgium; and when Arthur grew tired of the attentions of the aging poet, and threatened to leave him, Verlaine drew out a revolver and shot him in the wrist, and would have killed him if his hand had not been shaking.

At eighteen Arthur gave up writing poetry, and became a wanderer over the face of the earth. We have glimpses of him as a soldier of the Dutch army in Java, as a farmer in Alexandria, as a construction worker in Cyprus, as a circus performer in Hamburg, until he settled down as a gun runner and slave trader in Abyssinia. The last ten years of his life were devoted to acquiring a fortune in Abyssinia which would enable him to retire; but the fortune escaped him. He loved the torrential heat of the Abyssinian highlands, and wrote a steady series of reports on the geography and fauna of that little-known land, but they were reports that could have been written as well by any literate traveler. There was no more poetry in him, and if anyone asked him about his poems, which were being read in Paris, he would say they amounted to nothing, and sometimes he would add that poetry was "the wrong way." In his youth he looked like his father, handsome and ruddy-faced, with a fine forehead and eyes of a brilliant clear blue shot through with darker lights. He was tall and walked like a peasant. As he grew older, he came to resemble his pathetic, sharp-featured mother, and his youthful beauty vanished. He died of cancer in a hospital in Marseilles when he was about to return to the East. He was thirty-seven years old.

He hated Charleville with a consuming passion—one of his more pleasant names for the town was Carolopolmerdis—but nearly all his greatest poems were written there. Charleville has done its best to remember him. His birthplace, now a bookshop, has a plaque proclaiming him "poet and explorer." There is a small museum which houses a few of his manuscripts, some photographs and portraits. There is another plaque on the house where he wrote *Le Bateau Ivre*, and the street which borders on the Meuse, once called Quai de la Madeleine, is now called Quai Rimbaud. Unless they tore down the statue of the swashbuckling Prince Charles in the Place Ducale and substituted a statue of Rimbaud, they could hardly do greater honor to him.

The house where he wrote so many poems looks out on the white-columned mill and the dark, serenely flowing waters of the Meuse. It was very quiet there, with only a few children playing in the shadowy street. Like many others who have come here, I folded up a newspaper into a paper boat and watched it sail down the dark stream in memory of another boat launched on a violent sea. When Rimbaud wrote *Le Bateau Ivre* he had never seen the sea, but he wrote like the most ancient of mariners:

The Drunken Boat

As I descended Streams where no man goes,
I felt myself no longer led by haulers—
The screaming Redskins had taken them for targets,
And nailed them naked to the colored poles.

Little I cared for crews of any kind,
Carriers of Flemish grain or English cotton,
My troubles with the haulers all forgotten,
I wandered down the Streams my own sweet way.

Within the furious raging of the tides,
Heedless as a child I ran in winter weather!
And no unanchored headland ever knew
The wild triumphant uproar I have known.

The tempest blessed my vigils out to sea,
Light as a cork I danced upon the waves,
Who roll their victims through eternity,—
Ten nights I never missed the lanterns' idiot eyes!

Sweeter than sour apples to a child,
Green waters filled my piny cockleshell:
Stains of blue wine, vomitings, all was wild
To cleanse me, tear my grappling-iron and helm.

I have since bathed within the poem Sea
Star-seeped and milky-white and open-mouthed,
Green sky devouring, and sometimes I would see
A drowned man floating palely, lost in thought.

Delirium's blue fires were strangely tinted then,
And the slow pulsing in the violent sun,
Stronger than alcohol, vaster than your lyres
Ferment the freckled bitterness of love.

I have known the heavens split with lightning,
Surfs, currents, waterspouts, and evening drawing near,
And Dawn exalted like a nation of doves:
Sometimes I have seen what men believed they saw.

I have seen the low sun stained with mystic horrors,
Lit with long clots of purple color.
Like actors in an ancient play, the far-off waves
Opened and closed like shivering shutters.

On green nights I have dreamed of dazzling snows,
Slow kisses on the eyelids of the sea,
The circulation of unheard-of tides
And singing phosphors flaring blue and gold!

I followed for whole months the maddened waves,
The insane cattle charging at the reefs,
Nor ever dreamed the shining Virgins' feet
Could curb the muzzle of the panting Deep.

I've touched, you know, fantastic Floridas
Mingling flowers with human panthers' eyes!
And rainbows stretching out like bridles
To lead green sheep beneath the sea's horizons!

I saw the ferment of enormous marshes, nets
Where in the rushes a whole Leviathan rots!
Downfalls of water in the midst of calms,
Horizons cataracting into abysses!

Glaciers, silver suns, burning skies and pearly seas,
Contorted wrecks within the brown bay's depths,
Where giant serpents eaten up by vermin
Drop their black perfume from the twisted trees!

I would have shown children those gold horses
Of the blue waves, the golden fish that sing.
The foaming fish have blessed my wanderings.
Often a perfect wind has lent me wings.

Sometimes, tired martyr of the poles and tropics,
The sea, whose tossing made my sobbing sweet,
Raised me her dark flowers with yellow suckers,
And left me like a woman on her knees.

Peninsula, I tossed upon my shores
The strife and dung of brawling blond-eyed birds,

And sailed until, across my tattered rigging,
Drowned men came spinning backward to their sleep.

But I, lost boat in the cove's trailing hair,
Shot by the tempest into featherless air—
What Monitor, what Hansa ship could dredge
Up from the sea my carcass drunk with water?

Free, fuming, crowned with purple mists,
I gored the reddening heavens like a wall
Which bears the charming sweetmeats of good poets—
Lichens of the sun, the heaven's blue sweat;

Who, stained with moons electric, ran
Like a mad baulk, escorted by black seahorses
While Augusts with their cudgel blows tore down
The sea-blue skies, the flaming funnels there;

Who trembled, knowing that fifty leagues away
Behemoth roared and rutted in a whirlpool,
Eternal weaver of blue calms,
I long for Europe of the ancient parapets!

I have seen starry archipelagoes and isles
Whose delirious skies lie open to the wanderer:
—Do you sleep exiled in these depthless nights,
O million golden birds, O future vigor?

True I have wept too much. The Dawns are fearful.
All suns are bitter, and all moons are vile:
Sour love has swollen me with drunken stupors.
May my keel splinter! May I go down to sea!

Waters of Europe! Those I desire are the dark
And shivering pools where in the scented dusk
A sad and crouching child sets sail
A boat as frail as a May butterfly.

I can no longer, bathed in your languors, O Waves,
Wipe out the sea-wake of the cotton ships,
Nor yet confront the pride of flags and flames,
Nor swim beneath the slave-ship's dreadful eyes!

Virgin of Toulouse

Saint Louis,
polychrome statue
from Musée de Cluny

Saint Joan of Arc from fifteenth-century manuscript

Bronze Christ at Saint Sernin, Toulouse

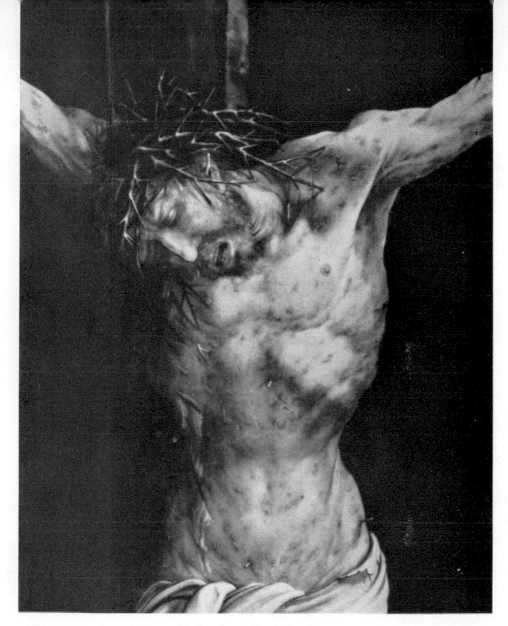

Christ, from Isenheim Altar

The Blue Virgin of Chartres

La Dame à la Licorne

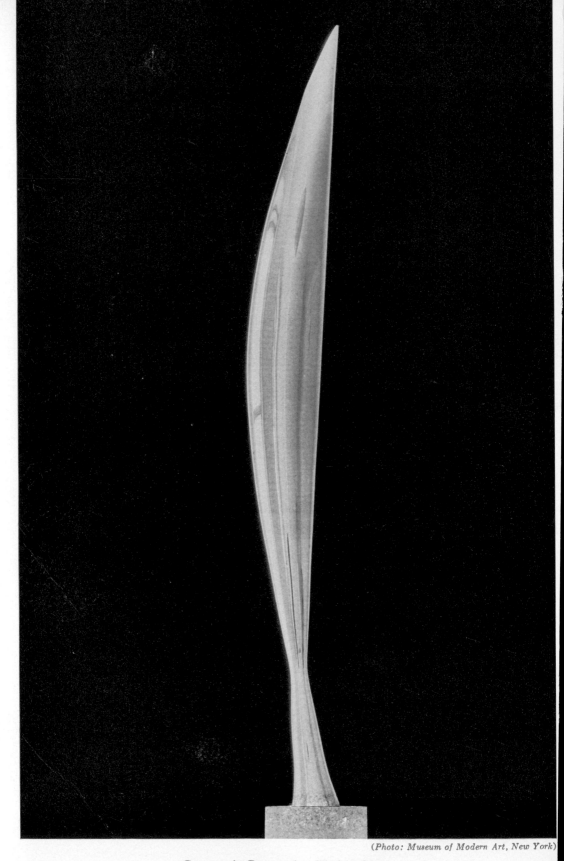

Constantin Brancusi: Bird in Space

So Rimbaud wrote in the crumbling house overlooking the Meuse only a month before his seventeenth birthday, when his career as a poet was nearly over. It was September and the leaves were beginning to fall and soon the cold northern winter would be on him. He wrote the poem as a means of escape from Charleville: it was to be his passport to the world of literary men in Paris. He seems never to have known or cared that it was his passport to immortality.

I watched the paper boat flowing down the silent Meuse, under the archways of the old mill, until, already waterlogged and crumbling, it vanished in the shadows, and then I turned up the long road which leads to one of the bleakest cemeteries in France, where Rimbaud was buried twenty years after writing *Le Bateau Ivre*.

The day had been warm and quiet, but now the cold rain came down, the sky darkening, the small sun making no shadows. It is an untidy cemetery situated on the brow of a hill, without any character at all, with crowded rows of stone angels and tilted tombstones, ugly and defiant in its ugliness. The rain came down and made a hissing sound as it fell on stone, and there was a sickly sweet smell in the air released by the rain. I found the grave, not far from the cemetery gate, on the brow of the hill. Here they had brought him on a bitter November day, when the wind was blowing fiercely across the Ardennes, six plumed black horses dragging his coffin up the hill, and the only mourners were the poet's mother and his sister Isabelle. It was a quick and hurried ceremony, for Madame Rimbaud had work to do on the farm.

The tombstone would have made him weep, with its florid cross and spray of white marble flowers, and under the name and date of his death is the inscription *Priez pour lui*. It is the kind of tombstone which was fashionable in the nineties of the last century, and Madame Rimbaud must have spent a good deal of money on it. There is a better memorial of him in the public park facing the railroad station: a head of the poet in green bronze turning his face sadly toward the city he wanted to flee.

Perhaps it would have been better if there were no memorial. Like Pascal and Racine, who are both lost somewhere beneath the stone floors of the church of Saint Etienne du Mont in Paris, though no one knows exactly where, he deserved a more mysterious resting place. He is among the greatest of Frenchmen. Before he was eighteen he had changed the course of French poetry. He had looked with fresh eyes at the colors of things, hurled himself at sensations, fought spiritual battles which left him wounded and incapable of living as other men lived, and he believed himself to be the forerunner of a new kind of man, the herald of a new race. He was the innovator, but he was the most traditional of poets, always celebrating divine clarity, in love with the sun and the fierce light of the heavens, writing in the last poem he ever wrote:

Why should we lament an eternal Sun, if we are engaged upon the discovery of divine clarity—far from the men who die upon the seasons?

Dawn will come at last, and then armed with a fiery patience we shall enter the splendid cities.

COLMAR

There are towns which seem to be suspended in a kind of no man's land, lost in mid-air, shadowless and changeless like a long winter's day. Those towns are often to be found on the borders far from the sources of power. They exist as though the world's events did not trouble them, as though modern inventions had never reached them, and the faces of the people have an untroubled quietness. These enviable people live out their rounded lives according to the seasons and die quietly of old age.

So it is in Colmar, the capital of Alsace, once a free city of the Holy Roman Empire under the Emperor Frederick II, now a small border town between Germany and France, living on its memories. History has poured through the town and left it curiously unaffected. The armies of Charles the Bold attacked it, and the Swedes swept up to its gates, and the Germans fought a last-ditch battle through its streets during the last war, but you would not guess there had been any fighting in the memory of man. With its gabled roofs and brightly painted houses and narrow winding streets, with flowerboxes on the window sills, it lives quietly in medieval magnificence. At night, in those cobbled streets, you have the feeling that the Holy Roman Empire is still in existence and at any moment armed horsemen with banners flying will come to attend midnight Mass.

Colmar is at its best on moonlight nights, when the gabled roofs turn misty silver and every cobblestone shines like a ghostly mirror. Through the narrow, winding streets of the old city the wandering lovers walk quietly, as though in an enchanted land. A drayhorse, suddenly emerging round a corner, will bring you immediately to the Middle Ages: in such a city automobiles seem purposeless, strange and imbecile, like magnified and carefully contrived insects, and the sight of a shop window filled with television sets comes like a shock on exposed nerves. Here, as in some remote towns in Italy, the illusion of the past is such that you enter the modern world only by an act of will. One could spend a lifetime in Colmar dreaming one's life away.

One day, walking through Colmar's old city, it occurred to me I had seen all these people before in Dürer's paintings and in *The Very Rich Hours* of the Duc de Berry. These people have the heaviness, the solidity and the grace of the Middle Ages, when the faces of the French and Germans were more similar than they are now. They walked unhurriedly, as people walk when they are lost in thought, and the passing traffic rarely rouses their attention. They live deeply within themselves, and their religious faith is still the center of their daily lives. They have the pride of the no-man's-landers, and like the Basques they form a kind of enclave, being perfectly aware of their difference from the rest of France. Above all the difference lies in their greater awareness of danger. To the people who live on the frontier Germany is an oppressive weight, a lurking fear.

Since in our own age we are all becoming no-man's-landers, there is something to be said for studying the people of Colmar, who have acquired techniques which we may have to learn. They have learned how to live quietly with their fears. They have learned over the centuries what it is like to be the plaything of the great powers. They know that ruin can fall on a beloved city in a moment of time. I talked to an old priest who was born when Alsace was German. "It is something you get accustomed to," he said. "For five hundred years we have been breeding fear out of us."

But it is not to study the no-man's-landers that visitors come flocking to Colmar. They come for the compelling reason that the city possesses nine separate masterpieces of painting, among them one *chef d'oeuvre* of such blazing authority that it must be counted among the wonders of the world. These nine paintings arc thc pancls of the Isenheim Altar in the Unterlinden Museum, a former Domini-can convent. They were painted about the year 1515 by Mathis Nithart, whose real name was forgotten for centuries, so that to this day he is known as Grünewald, following a mistake made by an art historian fifty years after his death. This mysterious painter, seemingly isolated from the currents of European art, painted more nakedly than anyone before him, or anyone since. He painted with fervent faith and a wild despair. Entering that cool and airy convent where the paintings are magnificently displayed, you are brought facc to facc with a living man dead for four hundred years.

Even today, though the art historians have been busy seeking some clues to explain his fantastic accomplishment, we know almost nothing about him. We have a glimpse of him in Joachim von Sandrart's gos-sipy account of the German painters of his age. "He led a lonely and melancholy life, and was unhappily married," we are told, and the statement rings true. He seems to have been born in Würzburg about the year 1478, and to have wandered disconsolately over the Rhine-land until he settled down for a while as court painter to the arch-bishop of Mainz, who permitted him the use of a coat of arms. They quarreled, and Nithart resumed his wanderings. One of the few cer-tain dates connected with his life is October 23, 1520, when he came to Aachen and visited Dürer, who was sufficiently impressed to present him with two florins' worth of engravings and woodcuts, a princely gift. By this time Nithart had completed his great altarpiece and taken service under Archbishop Albrecht von Brandenburg, who paid him regularly and gave him costly robes, furs and jewelry to wear. He died at Halle in 1528, and most of our knowledge about him is derived from the inventory of his estate, which lists among his possessions many valuable articles of clothing, much jewelry, "rare colors," books on hydraulic engineering and some Lutheran pam-phlets. He was soon forgotten, his paintings being attributed to others, his many names—for he seems to have taken a sardonic pleasure in hiding behind a multitude of names—becoming no name. He left an adopted son, who inherited his entire property; but of the son, as of the father, almost nothing is known.

Nithart hides in the shadows, a strange, imperturbable, passionate man, in love with bright-colored silks and everything glinting and flamelike, living on the borders of life, in those regions where the spirit and flesh are equally urgent and demanding, in uneasy alliance with one another. He walks solitary, as in a grave. His hands give him away, those hands which he painted in all the stages of prayer and adoration: hands which implore and cry out, hands that fold back upon themselves, hands like thorns. No one ever painted hands more delicately, or more menacingly. He will splay the fingers out, twist them in agony, crush them against one another, or give them such elegance and tenderness that we are compelled to look away from a face to watch the play of fingers. He gives gentleness and sorrow to the paw of the Lamb of God.

Nithart characteristically painted himself as Saint Sebastian on a panel to the right of his great Crucifix. It is the face of a man weighed down by sorrows, tight-lipped, unshaved, with an expression of intolerable yearning in the dark eyes gazing far into the distance. The hands are raised in prayer, but one hand lies in the hollow formed by the other; some mysterious significance seems to attach to the curious gesture. Saint Sebastian has the body of a peasant, with broad shoulders and strong legs, and round him, swirling like a red silken banner, is a cloak of many seams. This powerful, meditative figure seems unconcerned with the gaping wounds in his chest and the arrows embedded in his shoulder and right leg. Deliberately he turns away from the face of God.

But it is not the self-portrait which attracts your attention when you enter the bright chapel for the first time. The walls are white and spacious. Sunlight pours through high windows. The air streams over the stone floors and pours down from the vaulted roof. Outside the calm summer day is being prolonged; you can hear people walking in a nearby street and the distant sound of a tram bell. Suddenly it is darkest night, and everything is hushed and silent. In that dark night a single figure begins to glow.

There is a man nailed to a roughly formed cross, his thin arms stretched as though they could stretch no more, the fingers curled and crisped, some of them sharp as knives. A crown of needlelike thorns clusters haphazardly over the sunken, greenish head. The eyes are closed, but the mouth is open like a festering wound. Christ is in agony. A single flickering flame of consciousness, pouring through that green, emaciated and suppurating body, keeps the agony alive. Barbs from a whip have left thorns in the flesh, and the weals have turned bright orange. The flesh has gone from the legs: there is only muscle, and the broken envelope of flesh. A tattered and torn loin cloth, as tough as the bark of a silver birch tree, is wrapped loosely round the loins. The tormented feet are like crushed toads, with a ter-rifying life in them. There he hangs, and it is unthinkable that he will ever be lifted down from the cross. This is not the handsome, scarcely hurt youth who is displayed like a flag from so many Italian crosses. This is a crucifixion as it must have been; the fetid smell, the stretch-ing, the sagging. There is no comfort in this figure, who hangs against the darkest night, while an incandescent green lake gleams behind him. "Jesus will be in agony until the end of the world," wrote Pascal; and here the agony is made manifest, and the end of the world is still far away.

On one side of the cross a kneeling Mary Magdalene lifts up her anguished hands, her golden hair rippling over her orange-crimson gown, while on the other side the blood from the throat of the Lamb drips into a golden chalice. Standing above the Lamb, John the Bap-tist, who was dead at the time of the crucifixion, points a finger ten inches long at the figure of Jesus, with the words: ILLVM OPORTET CRESCERE ME AVTEM MINVI (He must increase but I must decrease) written above the hand in letters that glow faintly in the darkness; and it is beyond understanding why he should be there beside the windswept lake, or why he should be wearing a green sash tied in a lover's knot, but his presence is imaginatively so right that we ask no questions. Mary Magdalene prays vehemently, her rich garments seething with warm color, so that she comes to resemble a burning bush at the foot of the cross, and she too assumes a position which would seem to be completely impossible, unnatural and unreal, and yet we find ourselves accepting everything about her without a qualm. She glows, and her cheeks are red, and a flame quivers through her, while the Virgin by her side is pale as death, swooning in the arms of a young Saint John, who resembles a tow-haired student of theology, possessing no particular beauty. All these figures conspire to form a scene of hallucination and terror, which is felt immediately on the senses.

Nithart has painted the tremendous event as though he were a participant, standing no more than three feet away. His brooding presence is an almost tangible thing, as the painted figures are tangible. Air swirls round them, they breathe and have a life of their own, but it is not any life known on earth, nor does the light shining on them come from the sun. This mysterious light wells out of a mysterious darkness; it is the light of dreams and nightmares, the light that sometimes gleams in the dark corners of the soul.

What Nithart has done—it is one of the supreme miracles of European painting—is to paint the light that never was, and the darkness that is unimaginable, the experience of the day when there was darkness over all the earth. This dying Christ could never have been modeled on a corpse; it is something that must have sprung entire in the artist's imagination on a day of intense agony and intense faith. The ghastly green light, the flesh covered with sores, the putrefying wounds, the dry sweat, the watery blood, are seen with amazing lucidity, but they represent nothing that the human eye has ever seen. It is such a Christ as could only appear in visions.

All of the nine panels have this strange visionary quality, which sets them apart from the religious paintings of the time. Nithart was painting his *Crucifixion* at the same time that Raphael was painting the *Sistine Madonna;* they seem to be describing two entirely different religions. Nithart has the greater range. He can paint a choir of angels, setting them amid golden columns and under archways bursting with Gothic flowers, and make them completely credible. He will paint the Virgin in a summer landscape as she tenderly mothers her child with a wooden bathtub and a chamberpot at her feet, and nearby he will paint the same Virgin in a glow of incandescence so fierce, so burning that nothing is left of her except a white face, and red lips, and red eyes, and a crown of flames. In another panel, amid a swirl of flaming drapery, Christ ascends to Heaven, and he too is vanishing into incandescence, into a blazing aureole of fire through which we can distinguish faintly the features of an almost inconceivable majesty. The paintings of the dying Christ and the Christ rising in majesty complement each other, but there is an infinite distance between them. Nithart leaped across that gap as lightly as other men leap over a stone. He had reached a stage in which he was the complete master of his own vision. No one ever painted the divine splendor or the mortal agony with so great an assurance.

His demons in the panel depicting the temptation of Saint Anthony are only too real, altogether convincing. These demons are owls wearing the carapaces of lizards, cocks twisted in the shape of scorpions, horned griffins, bloated reptiles. Hieronymus Bosch will paint similar demons with disturbing power, but not with the sense of immediate and uncontrolled menace which leaps out of Nithart's painting. Here evil is made palpable, and is supreme. Tucked in the right-hand corner of the panel is a pathetic strip of parchment bearing the words: VBI ERAS JESV BONE VBI ERAS QVARE NON AFFVISTI VT SANARES VULNERA MEA (Where wert thou, good Jesus, where wert thou? Why didst thou not come to heal my wounds?). These words do not appear in the New Testament. They seem to have been forced out of Nithart himself as he watched with horrified fascination the power of evil to destroy the saints.

When all the panels have been seen, one returns again to the *Crucifixion* with the haunting sense that it might have vanished in the interval, for since the artist painted the imponderable and inconceivable, one hardly expects to enter that world for a second time. But it is still there, glowing richly and eerily; and as the afternoon is prolonged and the sun sets over the roofs of Colmar, the bright colors begin to fade, the scarlet robes turn to the color of rust, until at last you see only the white robes of the swooning Virgin and the heavy greenish gray of the towering Christ; and perhaps this too was intended—that Christ and the Virgin should come together at last.

This painting was commissioned by the Antonites of the small town of Isenheim near Colmar. A Sicilian, Guido Guersi, paid for it; some details of the iconography seem to have been provided by the Swedish mystic Saint Bridget; a Frenchman, Jean d'Orlier, was the prior of the monastery at Isenheim when it was being painted. Nithart, a German, himself seems to have been deeply influenced by

Burgundian painting. So many nations were involved in the making of it that the nationality of the painter becomes finally meaningless. The French quite properly regard it as one of their greater splendors.

They very nearly lost it during World War II. It was crated and put in a truck and sent to the Château de Lafarge near Limoges to prevent it from falling into the hands of the enemy. Limoges was reached safely, but along one of the country roads leading to the château the truck caught fire. The fire was put out before it reached the painting, with only a few seconds to spare. In 1794, during the French Revolution, a mob attempted to burn the altar, and it was saved by two men, Jean-Jacques Karpff and Jean-Pierre Marquaire, one a painter and the other a magistrate, who had been ordered by the Directory to make an inventory of paintings. Today there are a few faint cracks on the surface, but there are no other traces of its adventures, and the colors are as clear as on the day when Nithart finished it.

In a white chapel in Colmar you will enter Heaven and Hell, and because they are depicted with authority, you will come away singing.

THE ABBEY CHURCH
OF SAINT DENIS

She stands now ruined and faded, like an old one-eyed bitch begging for alms, though she was once the most beautiful woman in France. Her jewels are faded, and very few of them are left. Her clothes are patched, but here and there she wears some of the finery she wore when she was young. Once she was a queen among queens, but age and the smoke of factories have blackened her, and she has been mutilated beyond repair, though there still lingers about her a hint of her former loveliness. She was the royal mother of Gothic cathedrals everywhere, and no other church in Christendom shone with such magnificence and splendor.

In the twelfth century the Abbey Church of Saint Denis was a jewel casket of blinding colors. The doors were of bronze sheeted with hammered gold; the altar and all the holy vessels were of purest gold; the windows blazed with colored glass. The relics of the martyrs were enclosed in jewel-studded reliquaries of a blinding brilliance, befitting the presence of the patron saint of France, who according to the legend had received communion from the hands of Christ. There was no holier place in France than this shrine to Saint Denis. For this reason the French kings were buried here, and here they came in time of war to receive from the abbot the sacred banner of the kingdom, the *oriflamme*, with its golden flames on a scarlet ground, which was displayed in the sanctuary in time of peace. Here Joan of Arc, wounded in battle, came to offer up the mysterious sword she received from Saint Catherine and the pure white banner emblazoned with the fleur-de-lys and the figure of the Saviour.

For eleven centuries the Abbey Church was the sacred vessel through which all French history seemed to pass. It was sacked during the French Revolution: the stained glass windows were smashed, the heads of the statues were struck off, and the treasure was dispersed. There remained little more than the empty shell.

Today few visitors come to see the church, though it is easy enough to reach by bus and métro. They do not come, because the slums crowd round it on all sides, and on all except the brightest days this suburb of Paris presents an aspect of inexpressible misery and poverty. The poor shuffle past the church without pausing to look up at the bronze doors on which the famous Abbot Suger can be seen kneeling at the feet of Christ during the Last Supper. There is so much poverty in Saint Denis that for generations the people have elected Communists to office. The most lovely product of the Middle Ages is a scorched island in the midst of industrial desolation.

Still she remains, and the few who visit her go away with a sense of incredulity, for it is still possible to be transported into a twelfth-century fairyland. The stained glass windows still glow, the columns soar cleanly to the heavens, the tombs of the kings are here in profusion, and in the crypt are the bones of Saint Denis.

As for Saint Denis, he was the strangest saint ever to march headless through the streets of Paris. From the very beginning there was something improbable about him, and there is even some doubt whether he ever existed. All we know for certain is that from about A.D. 650 it was firmly believed that his relics reposed beneath a church erected in his honor. According to the legend he came from Rome about four hundred years before, accompanied by his two companions Rusticus and Eleutherius, to preach the Gospel to the Gauls, and after many years of ministering to the people of Paris he was suddenly arrested by the Roman governor, thrown into prison, tortured and executed at Montmartre, the mount of the martyrs. Thereupon he calmly picked up his head, carried it to a fountain where he washed the face, and cradling his head in his arms he set out for a long walk across the open fields. And then, about 800, Dionysus the martyr became strangely confused with Pseudo-Dionysius the Areopagite who wrote in Greek about the nature of the heavenly light and the powers of the angels.

Saint Denis is all mystery and perplexity, darkness and sudden gleams of light. We see him only faintly, moving like a ghost through misty streets when Paris was surrounded by marshes and ice floes floated down the Seine. It is a pity we know him so little, for he was the first bishop of Paris, the first evangelist to the Gauls, and the patron saint of France.

But while Saint Denis remains mysterious, there is no mystery at all about Abbot Suger, who built the royal church of Saint Denis and wrote a book describing every detail of its construction and how he accumulated a vast treasure to pay for it. We know what he looked like, for he was an imperious man, determined to be remembered, and he ordered a stained glass window showing himself lying prone at the feet of the Virgin—he is almost the same size as the Virgin, and he has written his name in letters which are exactly as large as the name of the Virgin. He was not a handsome man. He had a heavy, powerful, oxlike face, with a low brow, enormous eyes and pendulous cheeks—he might be taken for a dock worker. His mouth attracts attention, for it is taut and lean and very long, the mouth of a man who gives orders and expects them to be obeyed.

Almost single-handedly Abbot Suger, the son of a serf, brought Gothic art into existence. He it was who filled the churches with light and sent the slender columns spinning so high they seem to be reaching to the foothills of heaven. He shattered the walls to let the light in, and gilded the altar so that it would shine like the sun. For him all light was heavenly, being God's breath made visible, and the radiance of the angels. So he built a church like a cascade of jewels, a fountain of emeralds and rubies, a lake of silver and gold, to bring people nearer the heart of the glowing mystery of light. He built a church in the form of a treasure casket of jewels flashing in God's holy fire.

He knew very well what he was doing, for he left thirteen separate inscriptions celebrating his achievements in stone and bronze. There is not the faintest trace of humility in these inscriptions. He storms the gates of Heaven and demands a place in Paradise as a reward for building a church so beautiful.

> *O Great Denis, throw open the gates of Paradise,*
> *And grant unto Suger thy holy protection.*
> *Mayest thou, for whom I have built thy new dwelling-place,*
> *Receive me into a dwelling place in Heaven,*
> *That I may eat to the full at the heavenly table.*

Not content with demanding the intervention of Saint Denis, he makes the same demand from Christ, the Virgin, Saint Paul and the angelic hosts, always invoking the splendor of his church as his passport to immortality. *Splendor, claritas, nobilitas* are words he uses constantly, and sometimes the words trip over one another, as on the inscription of the great bronze doors:

> *Whoever seeks to praise the glory of these doors,*
> *Let him not marvel at the golden treasure but at the workmanship.*
> *Bright is the noble work: this work shining nobly*
> *Enlightens the mind so that it may travel through the true lights*
> *To the True Light where Christ is the true door.*

Nobile claret opus. . . . Bright is the noble work. . . . Such is his theme, and it is not one which he ever permitted himself to lose sight of. Not only must everything be made to glow with inexpressible brilliance, but there must be a constant exchange and marriage of lights, each object shedding light on all the other objects and in all directions. It was not sufficient to cover the altar with sheets of gold at front and sides, but the back too must be covered with gold, and all the objects on the altar must also be gilded. He found in a chest belonging to the church a long-forgotten antique porphyry vase of a rich purple color. It was a very simple vase. For Suger it was far too simple and unpretentious to appear on the altar, and accordingly he transformed it into a golden eagle, with an elaborate superstructure formed of wings and claws and a long neck surmounted by an astonishingly imperious head. This golden eagle is an expression of pure power. There is no gentleness in it. It has a Byzantine elegance, and it still has some of the roughness we associate with Romanesque. There is no straining after effect. This eagle with the impossibly long neck demands and receives our respect; and if it could speak it would utter words of resounding authority, filling the whole church with the menace of its voice. Even today, when it stands in a glass case in the Louvre, no more than ten or eleven inches high, the golden eagle still triumphantly asserts its power. On the collar can be seen the words: *Marmor erat.* "It *was* marble," Suger proclaims, "but it is marble no more." He seems to have designed the eagle himself, for his name "Sugerius" is engraved on a silver plate beneath the porphyry vase.

The golden eagle is an expression of royal power divorced from Christian feeling. The cruel beak, the hooded eyes, the great talons, the neck with its eleven rows of cusped feathers suggest controlled ferocity, but they also suggest splendor, clarity and nobility. Suger has transformed a simple vase into flaming majesty.

He did exactly the same thing with a sardonyx chalice which came into his possession. The rich black and purple-red of the sardonyx were insufficient for his shining purpose. It must be given an ornamental setting of gold and silver and rare stones. About the top of the chalice he placed a ribbon of pearls and rubies, and the pedestal too was encrusted with jewels and rich *repoussé* work, and there must be handles by which the chalice can be lifted. These handles are perhaps the most amazing additions, for they have the curve of a bent bow and possess an exquisite grace and rightness. In the chalice Suger was able to combine barbaric strength with an almost Florentine delicacy. It is a strange and dazzling work, such as one might find among the treasures in a great chieftain's tomb, and there is no doubt that this is the effect he intended. This formidable chalice—one of the few surviving works of art known to have been fashioned at his command—vanished at the time of the French Revolution. Rediscovered in 1922, it now belongs to the National Gallery of Art in Washington.

Suger believed as an article of faith that only the most beautiful and costly objects would serve to decorate the place of God and the martyred Saint Denis, and therefore it was incumbent upon him to ransack all France for jewelry. From the king came gifts of emeralds, from Count Thibault of Champagne came hyacinths and rubies, and every nobleman at court was compelled to pay a tribute of jewels. On one famous occasion when he was in desperate need of jewels and none seemed to be available, he offered up a prayer, and the inevitable miracle happened, for some time later a deputation of monks arrived from Citeaux with an offer to sell him some precious stones, and soon two more deputations came until he was almost surfeited with emeralds, rubies, topazes, sapphires and amethysts, "such as I could not have dared to hope to see in ten years." He paid four hundred pounds for a mountain of precious stones and thought himself doubly blessed for having acquired them so cheaply.

What is surprising is that Suger succeeded in amassing all this treasure at a time when so many churchmen were inveighing against the ostentation in churches. "What has gold to do with the sanctuary?" Bernard of Clairvaux thundered. "Look how the Church inlays the stones of her cathedrals with gold, while leaving her sons naked!" Suger was bitterly attacked by Bernard, and he seems to have known that he could give no logical explanation for this thirst for treasure, so he replied with a theory that jewels in themselves conferred no benefits on God or on His worshipers, and perhaps their very existence was to be deplored, but how brightly they shone! with what dazzling brilliance they reflected the holy light of the sun! how delightful it was to gaze upon them and to be transported into a realm above the dust of the world! and surely the majesty of God should be celebrated with majestic ritual and majestic implements! Bernard of Clairvaux, the pure ascetic, could make nothing of these arguments, and he seems to have retired from the combat with the feeling that Suger was a law to himself and nothing could be done to prevent him from carrying out his ambition of making the Abbey Church of Saint Denis the most sumptuous in the world.

Suger firmly believed that Dionysus the Roman martyr who died at Montmartre and the Greek scholar known as Dionysius the Areopagite were the same person. In his mind the man who walked headless across the open fields and the man who wrote an intellectual treatise on the heavenly light were inseparable. It was a belief that was common at the time, though violently disputed by Abélard. There were reasons—very odd reasons—to support this belief. In A.D. 827 the Byzantine Emperor Michael the Stammerer sent an embassy to Louis the Pious, the son of Charlemagne, bearing magnificent gifts including the complete works of Dionysius the Areopagite supposed to be written in his own hand. They reached Paris on the eve of the feast day of Saint Denis. Nineteen miracles occurred in quick succession. These miracles, the similarity of the names, and the accident of their arrival on the eve of the feast day combined to suggest that the holy writings of the martyr had come to join his holy relics. The manuscripts of Dionysius the Areopagite were placed in the keeping of Hilduin, abbot of Saint Denis. Three hundred years later, when Suger was abbot, they were still there. Suger was deeply learned in the works of Dionysius the Areopagite. He venerated the relics of Saint Denis. Believing with passionate ardor in Saint Denis, martyr and Areopagite, he determined to rebuild the Abbey Church in a way which would please both a patron saint and the scholar who believed in the holiness of light. Out of this singular succession of accidents emerged the purity of Gothic architecture.

It is a strange story and we shall understand it better if we assume that the French came to believe in the holiness of light because they wanted to believe it, because the belief was already present in the air of France. When Dionysius the Areopagite wrote that "every creature, visible or invisible, is a light brought into being by the Father of Lights," he was saying something which was immediately intelligible to the French mind. All through French history we are made aware of light as a fluid or a vapor bathing and penetrating all things, palpable and sweet like fruit. "God is an overflowing radiance, illuminating with His fullness every mind above the world, around it, or within it, and thereby renewing their spiritual powers." Or again, listen to Dionysius the Areopagite as he describes God's holy fire in a passage which seems to have been written with a full orchestra:

This fire is in all things, is spread everywhere, pervades all things without intermingling with them, shining by its very nature and yet hidden, and manifesting its presence only when it finds material on which to work, violent and invisible, having absolute rule over all things, violently assimilating to itself everything it triumphantly seizes, and so renewing all things with its life-giving heat and blazing with inextinguishable light; never defeated, unchangeable, darting upon its prey, changeless always, as it lifts that which it gathers to the skies, never held back by any servile baseness, self-moved, moving other things. It comprehends, but remains incomprehensible, never in need, mysteriously increasing itself, and showing forth its majesty according to the nature of the substance receiving it, powerful and mighty and invisibly present in all things.

Suger was determined that the glowing of the holy fire should be present in his church; and the supreme evocation of the holy fire took the form of immense jewel-like rose windows. Then, for the first time in history, these great flaming wheels of light came into existence. These roses are the supreme gift of Gothic to our time. There, as Dante says, *la luce divina è penetrante per l'universo secondo ch'è degno*—"the divine light penetrates the universe according to its dignity."

Intoxicated with light, drunk with visions, Suger presided over the fortunes of Saint Denis until the end. Though ill, he would rise from his narrow cot in his narrow cell, and drag his "imbecile body" (*imbecille corpus*) to take part in the services of the church, haunting the church which he had built to the greater glory of the Father of Lights, until at last at the age of seventy he died, worn out by his exertions, in the middle year of the twelfth century.

His spirit remains exceedingly alive. Almost single-handed he invented Gothic, and the great Gothic churches to be found all over France bear the trace of his influence. The Abbey Church of Saint Denis served as their model. Saint-Germain-des-Prés, Chartres, Vézelay and fifty more churches are indebted to him, for they are all the daughters of that smoke-begrimed church now rotting away in a dreary industrial suburb of Paris.

CHARTRES

About the time that Abbot Suger was dying in Saint Denis, an un-known sculptor of remarkable originality and power was carving the figures on the west portal at Chartres. He was one of the greatest sculptors the world has ever seen, and he was almost certainly trained at Saint Denis, but everything about him and about the sculptures he made remains mysterious. Where did he come from? What other sculptures did he make? What do these sculptures represent? Why were they made to join mystically with the vertical architecture of the façade? We do not know the answers to any of these questions.

These long imperial figures who guard the royal gate at Chartres have no names, and even now after centuries of probing among ancient manuscripts we are no nearer a solution of their origin. Some claim they are the ancestors of Christ, others that they are portraits of kings and queens of France, and still others believe they are saints of venerable antiquity. They stand there in a strange time-worn quietness, seeming to be not of our time, nor of any time. Shepherds or kings or saints, they are lost in dreams of blessedness.

In all of France there are no statues to compare with these dreaming figures who guard the royal gate with a kind of *abandonnement*. Like the Caryatids of the Erechtheum they give the impression that at any moment they will walk out from under their stone canopies and desert the temple forever. They do not belong to the world. Their robes are rippled like the surface of a pool when a stone is flung into it, and these mysterious folds seem to widen into infinity, yet they have the calm of still waters. The stone is muddied with bird droppings and here and there blackened with soot, but neither the birds nor the soot nor the poisonous chemicals in the air can disturb their composure, the perfection of their peace. They are not angels nor divinities, for something human still attaches to them; and perhaps they are not even kings and queens, nor ancestors of Christ, nor saints. There they remain, remote and immutable, like strangers to our own time. It is simpler perhaps to regard them as aspects of divine grace.

Those nineteen figures at the gate have survived by a miracle. They survived the great fire of 1194 only because they had been detached and removed some twenty feet away before the fire broke out. A few are damaged. One has lost its head completely; another, which once bore the head of a young man, now wears the head of a young girl, and under her feet a man entwined by two serpents is most mysteriously being trodden down. Next to her stands a regal figure, his feet resting on a woman, who lightly fingers the tresses of her long hair, while clutching the tail of a dragon in her free hand. Then below the third figure of the group we find a toad, a dog, a large ape, two dragons and a basilisk with a monkey's face. It is all mystery. We do not know what is happening, and can only guess that these figures have the power to keep Hell at bay.

The men raise their hands in blessing—hands which have vanished—and some hold the scepters and instruments of power, while the women hold books and gaze tranquilly into the future, wielding no power except prophecy. All smile their ghostly smiles, save for one with swelling breasts and two long plaits over her shoulders who smiles with happy impudence, and therefore it has been assumed that she is Mary Magdalene or the wayward Queen Clotilde. I suspect that she is as nameless as the rest, and she is there because a happy impudence is one of the aspects of divine grace.

The cathedral was burned to the ground in 1134, and it was burned again sixty years later. At some period between the two fires these sculptures were made: it is possible that they were made about the year 1144 during that period when all of northern France was seized with religious fervor. Robert de Torigny, the prior of the abbey of Mont Saint-Michel, was only one of many witnesses who reported on the events of that extraordinary year. "In this same year," he wrote, "the men of Chartres harnessed themselves to cartloads of stone and wood, and pulled carts laden with grain or whatever else was required for the building of the cathedral. It was the time when the towers were soaring skyward, and the like of these times were never seen again. The enthusiasm spread through the whole of France and Normandy. Everywhere penance and humility prevailed, and everyone forgave his enemies. Everywhere men and women were dragging heavy loads through the swamps. Singing in triumph beneath the lash and thong they praised the miracles performed by God before their eyes."

So Chartres was built, and it is unthinkable that it should have been built in any other way.

THE BLUE VIRGIN

Among the stained glass windows at Chartres there is one so beautiful and awe-inspiring that for centuries candles were lit before it and offerings were made to it. This was the window of the Blue Virgin. Today her place has been usurped by the Virgin of the Pillar, who is small and doll-like, wrapped in brocaded vestments, seeming to float amid a sea of candles beside the entrance to the choir. Though she was carved in the thirteenth century, she is a newcomer, her worship being intimately connected with the proclamation of the doctrine of the Immaculate Conception in 1855. Unknown and unworshiped before the proclamation of the doctrine, she suddenly emerged as the most numinous of all the representations of the Virgin, the protectress of the cathedral, the giver of blessings, the one carried in processions. She shines in the light of a thousand candles. The Blue Virgin, being made of glass, is content to shine in the light of the sun.

The Blue Virgin is a figure of authentic majesty. She survived the great fire of 1194 and belongs to the time when people harnessed themselves to carts and dragged the quarried stone to the site with a sense of exultant joy in their handiwork, at the very beginning of the cathedral. The date of the window is about 1150, while the greater part of the remaining glass dates from between 1215 and 1240. She therefore represents the Virgin as she appeared in the minds and spirits of her worshipers when her worship was still new in France. For her they built this house so that she should have a worthy residence.

The freshness of the dawn is in that window, but it is not a dawn that ever lit the skies of France. Scarlet and crimson and ruby-red have filled that flaming oriental sky with their fiery glow. She comes from the East, bringing with her the colors of an eastern sky. From Byzantium or Jerusalem she has come, and there is about her more than a suggestion that she is a stranger in the land, not yet accustomed to these northern climes. Clad in bright vestments of translucent blue, she is seen against an eternal sunrise, gazing at the beholder with the faintest inclination of her head. The inclination suggests assent, and is peculiarly French, for the Byzantine Madonnas never permit their heads to lean to one side, nor do they ever wear a halo of the purest blue, the color of the cloudless skies. Such a blue halo was seen by the peasant girl at Lourdes when the Virgin appeared to her.

She sits there on a jeweled throne, attended by her angels, with the Christ Child on her lap, and she is so calm against the flaming heavens that she gives an impression of being remote from them, and indeed of being very close to the worshiper, leaning forward a little as though about to descend from her glittering throne. She is robed majestically, but she wears her majesty lightly. There is a heavy jeweled crown upon her forehead and her features are framed in a golden veil, but the stiffness of veil and crown vanishes in the rippling folds of her gown, the color of a summer lake when the wind roughens its surface. There is no scepter, no emblem of power, unless it is the brilliant ring-necked dove descending from the heavens above her crown. So she gazes from her window in blue and gold, very calm, mingling Byzantine majesty with a peculiarly French gentleness and grace, while the hurrying angels swing censers at her head and feet and others bring candles to light her on her way.

The impression conveyed by the Blue Virgin is one of quite extraordinary peace arising from the intense purity of the blue light flooding over her; it is only later, after looking at her for some while, that you realize how complex are the forces which have brought this peace into existence. The Virgin is unmoving, but all round her there is ceaseless activity. The angels swing their censers high above their heads, their rainbow-colored wings are tossed in all directions, their robes are swirling in the winds of heaven. There is activity, even violent activity, within the contours of the Virgin herself, for the Christ Child on her lap is seething with explosive life, and this life comes from the extraordinarily involved abstract design of his robes made up of wedges of mauve, purple, chocolate, rust-red, yellow and sudden bright glimpses of green, like those liquid greens which flare and flash in oriental sunsets. The head, the halo, the feet, an upraised hand and the book of the Gospels are clearly visible, but all the rest forms a powerful abstraction which, if it can be compared with anything at all, resembles a sliced pomegranate. The Christ Child is all furious energy and controlled confusion. He is the whirlwind proclaiming the scholastic words, while the Mother proclaims majestic tenderness.

Nowhere else in the cathedral, not even in the sculptured figures of the *portail royal* which are contemporary with her is there anything to compare with her in majesty. The great rose window, called the Rose of France, dedicated to the Virgin and offered to the cathedral by Saint Louis, glows and crackles like a bonfire, but the central medallion of the Virgin is too small, and too obscure, to receive the tribute due to majesty. The colors of the rose window are aristocratic, not royal. Light pours through the rose like a fountain in the sunlight: the light which pours through the Blue Virgin comes in a steady imperial glow.

Deliberately the Blue Virgin was placed low on the walls, to enable her to step down whenever she pleased to walk in her royal courts. Being so low, within human reach, the wonder is that she endured so long. These splinters of glass are paper-thin: a strong wind or a handful of stones could smash her to smithereens. During the French Revolution a statue of the Virgin in the choir was adorned with a red cap and a pike was thrust into her hands, while a mountain of earth was erected close to her to support a statue of Reason. Plays were performed, and every tenth day, the revolutionaries' Sunday, wild dances were held in the nave. Four stained glass windows perished in the Revolution, but the Blue Virgin remained unharmed. She was dismantled during World War I and hidden away in a château south of Paris, and in World War II she was dismantled again, but there was no time to remove her to a safe hiding place in the south of France. Crated, lying in a bed of straw, she was taken down to the crypt. The Germans searched for her and never found her, for she lay behind a dummy wall in the furthermost regions of the crypt until the war was over.

The adventures of the Blue Virgin were few compared with the adventures of the Virgin's Veil, the *sancta camisia*, which is kept in a gilded reliquary behind the high altar. This veil of raw silk, which has yellowed with age, was said to have been given by the Byzantine empress Irene to Charlemagne, whose grandson Charles the Bald gave it into the keeping of Chartres about the year 876. Kings and princes vied with one another to heap jewels upon the casket which enclosed the veil: to lay hands upon the casket, to walk underneath it, to be permitted to kiss its crystal window were honors reserved only to potentates. So much wealth accumulated around the veil that it was said to equal the entire revenue of France in a single year.

Today you can still see the veil, or rather a portion of it, for during the French Revolution it vanished, and when found again only about half of it remained. It must have been a very large veil, for the remaining half measures six feet by ten feet. It lies in a cedar coffer, and through a glass window you can see the thin folded edges of the silk glinting brightly, the yellow turning to gold. The severely intellectual prelate who is in charge of the reliquary smiles tolerantly. "We do not know whether it is truly the veil of the Virgin," he will say. "We only know that for eleven hundred years men have thought it so."

THE RED HAND

As you walk away from the cathedral, no more than a hundred yards from the west portal you come upon a grass slope. It is a small slope with a white wall behind it, with nothing remarkable about it except that a monstrous and massive hand of polished red stone rises out of the grass, clutching a sword. The hand is bleeding and the sword is broken.

This small slope of grass is also a sacred place. Buried beneath the grass are the ashes of hundreds of resistance fighters killed by the Germans. The ashes were removed from the prison at Fresnes and from Père Lachaise cemetery. On the white wall the name of JEAN MOULIN has been carved in immense letters. It is his memorial and his ashes are buried here, but it is also a memorial for the resistance fighters everywhere in France.

Jean Moulin was a small dark man with a wide mouth and laughing eyes, born in Béziers in the south of France, who looked like a young mechanic, but was in fact a brilliant administrator. In 1940, at the time of the collapse of France, he was Prefect of Chartres. Ordered by the Germans to sign a declaration that the corpses lying around Chartres were the victims of French atrocities, he refused. He was arrested and tortured, and when he could bear the torture no longer and was afraid he would submit to the enemy, he cut his own throat. The Germans seem to have possessed a strange respect for him, for they took him to a hospital, brought him back to life, and on his recovery ordered that he be received with military honors. In September 1941 he escaped to England.

For a long time Moulin was hardly to be distinguished from all the other French officers surrounding General de Gaulle in London. It was observed that he was unusually quiet and unusually gifted in administrative matters, but no one yet expected him to show powers of leadership. It was thought that he was too slight, too intellectual, too deeply wounded to be a resistance leader. Moulin thought otherwise. He had a vast knowledge of the resistance movements in France, for he was able to study all the reports filtering into London. General de Gaulle was impressed with his assessments, and at last in April 1943 Moulin and General Delestraint were given sweeping powers to reorganize the resistance forces. Secretly they entered Vichy France and made their way into occupied territory. Soon Delestraint was arrested, and Moulin was left in sole command. He went under two names—"Max" and Jacques Martel. The Germans put a price on his head.

For two months Max traveled all over occupied France, reorganizing resistance groups, arranging for equipment to be dropped by para-chute, setting up secret radio transmitters, and fighting a curious and continual battle with the French Communists, who took orders from Moscow and not from De Gaulle. One day in June he was arrested in a village near Lyons and taken to the German headquarters. No one suspected his identity. The Germans had simply rounded up a group of Frenchmen at random, and Max was among them. Photo-graphs of the prisoners were taken and sent to Paris. Someone in Paris remembered the Prefect of Chartres and guessed that Max might be Jean Moulin. Then, in the Fort de Montluc in Lyons, the calvary of Jean Moulin began.

When the Germans were in full retreat from France, General de Gaulle ordered a full inquiry into the fate of his trusted lieutenant. It was possible to reconstruct his last days in precise detail. At two o'clock in the afternoon of June 23 the door of his cell opened and he was led out for examination. The German security police officer was a man called Barbie, a heavy-set man with a ferocious temper.

"We know everything," said Barbie. "You are Max. You are Jacques Martel. You are Jean Moulin."

Moulin refused to speak. He was beaten, pummeled, tortured, thrown down steps, and he never opened his mouth. Once he was given a sheet of paper and ordered to describe the organization of the secret resistance army. Instead he drew a caricature of Barbie. En-raged, Barbie tortured him again. There were three days of torture, and Moulin was already dying when orders were received to take him to security headquarters at 84 Avenue Foch in Paris. Hauptsturm-führer Barbie himself drove the car to Paris, with Moulin propped up in the back seat. He thought he had done well and would be complimented for capturing and torturing a dangerous enemy, but his superiors thought otherwise. Moulin was too important to kill; he should be kept alive in the hope that he would be induced to talk. Accordingly Barbie was punished, and the security officers did every-thing they could to revive Moulin, removing him to a private hospital in Neuilly, hovering over him like guardian angels, while a stream of telegrams was dispatched between Berlin and Paris. One day when Moulin seemed to be recovering, a German officer entered his hospital room and showed him a slip of paper on which his name had been written: JEAN MOULLIN. Moulin smiled wearily and scratched out the second "l." He had the French passion for exactitude.

It was decided to take him to Berlin, for Ribbentrop and Kaltenbrunner were showing an uneasy interest in the fate of the appointed leader of the French resistance. It was hoped that under the care of German doctors he would revive sufficiently to be tortured again into revealing his knowledge of the plans of the Allies. On the morning of July 8 he was lifted into a special compartment of a train at the Gare de l'Est. When the train reached Metz he was in a coma, and he seems to have died just about the time the train entered Germany. For some reason the body was returned to Paris. He was cremated and the ashes were placed in Père Lachaise cemetery. They were found after the war only because the Germans meticulously numbered all the urns. The urn containing the ashes of Jean Moulin was numbered 10,137. He was only forty-four at the time of his death. Years later General de Gaulle said: "If he had lived, he would have become the first postwar Prime Minister of France."

In Chartres there are two great monuments. One is the cathedral, and the other is a patch of bright green grass.

VINCENNES

Here and there in France you will come upon towers of exquisite shape and nobility. The Tour de Constance at Aigues-Mortes is one of them, a dazzling thing shaped like a Saracen's helmet. There are great towers at Villandraut and at the Château de Bonaguil, but these are far from the beaten path. Paris was once a forest of towers, but all have gone except the Tour Saint Jacques, venerable and unlovely as a decayed tooth. But very close to Paris, in the Bois de Vincennes, you come upon a tower of majestic proportions and the color of old gold, which has hardly changed since it was built by Charles V in the fourteenth century.

In the Bois de Vincennes the saintly King Louis IX used to hold court under an oak tree. It was wild country, thick with forests where the deer wandered and the wolves hid in the high grass and the wild boars raged. From very early times the French kings had their country estates here in a clearing in the forest. The castle seems to have been a simple house made of wood, surrounded by the wooden pavilions of the courtiers, until the time of Philippe le Bel, the silent, handsome king who gazed at all men with a curiously fixed expression of the eyes. He was the first of the Valois, and he trusted no man; least of all did he trust the Parisians who rose in rebellion against him. So he gave orders that a stone fortress should be built where previously there was a small rustic estate. The work was completed by

Charles V, called Charles the Wise for no reason which any historian has been able to discover. He also built the Bastille.

Eight great towers were built, joined by a curtain wall. Of these towers the highest was 170 feet high, a stone keep of fierce proportions and exquisite simplicity. The Tour de Constance does not impress with its power; the keep at Vincennes does. It says in the simplest possible way what had to be said. It proclaims the king's majesty and hurls defiance at the world.

This keep has the simplicity of a modern skyscraper and is no more than an immense oblong box with circular towers at each corner. Architecturally it derives its strength from the absolutely right proportions of the towers to the box, and the way the seventeen-feet-thick walls are broken up by a few widely spaced and menacing windows. Not even the great fortress castles of Apulia suggest such controlled energy and power.

We know what the keep looked like soon after it was built because it is included among the paintings of *The Very Rich Hours* of the Duc de Berry. Jean de France, Duc de Berry, was the brother of Charles V, and one of the luckiest and most rapacious men who have ever lived. He had excellent taste, and, being perhaps the wealthiest man in all of France, he chose to satisfy his taste to the utmost. In 1409, when he was nearly seventy, he announced that he wanted to have the most beautiful book of hours ever painted to supplement a collection which already included twenty books of hours. Three brothers, Pol, Hermant and Hennequin de Limbourg, were commissioned to make the paintings. The Duc de Berry commanded that these superb miniaturists should paint all the duke's palaces and castles, of which he had accumulated sixteen in a long lifetime. Among these castles was Vincennes, where the duke had been born, though at his birth the building of the great towers had only just begun. In the painting the towers gleam above the forest in the setting sun, white-gold and very delicate, as seen from a great distance. It is perhaps the best way to represent them, for seen at a shorter range they only show their appalling power.

Jean de Berry had a mania for collecting. He collected castles, books, jewelry, gold vessels and holy relics in extraordinary profusion, and since he was constantly traveling from one castle to another, and taking with him his most precious objects, he was always accompanied by a private army of a thousand men. His treasures included a whale's tooth, many ostrich eggs, the jaw of a fossilized giant, and the horn of a unicorn. His most holy relics were the wedding ring of Joseph and a milk tooth which had once belonged to the Virgin. He owned a copy of the Gospel of Saint John written on parchment, which was curious only because the entire volume was about the size of a penny piece. He was a heavy, thickset, ugly man with a florid color and a permanent expression of petulance; and being one of those men who bring about revolutions and deserve to be assassinated, he died in bed, in the odor of sanctity, at the age of seventy-six, and was buried among the kings at Saint Denis.

He did not however die in good humor, for in 1415, the year before his death—it was the year in which the Limbourg brothers painted for him the towers of Vincennes in *The Very Rich Hours*—all France was shaken by the catastrophe of Agincourt, where a small body of English archers under Henry V destroyed the flower of the French nobility. The English lost a few hundred, the French had ten thousand men killed. All northern France fell into the hands of the English, and the Duc de Berry lost most of his castles.

Seven years later Henry V was journeying to Paris to be crowned king of France when he died at Vincennes, in the great upper room where the arms of England are still painted on the walls. He had married a French princess, and a child had been born to them. He was forty years of age, but as he lay dying he looked like an old man, and no one would have recognized in him the impetuous Prince Hal. His body swollen, his face turning black, he died slowly. On August 31, 1422, he called to his doctors and ordered them to tell him the truth, and they knelt before his couch and whispered that at most he could only hope for two or three more hours of life. Then his confessor stepped forward and began to read the seven penitential psalms, and Henry shouted the words; and when he came to the words *ut aedificantur muri Jerusalem,* he paused and announced to all those who were standing around the deathbed that if God spared him he would lead a crusade to the Holy Land, and he was still reading the psalms when he died.

A few weeks later the Duke of Bedford, Henry's brother, acting as regent for the infant King Henry VI, was solemnly showing to the people the Crown of Thorns from the steps of the Sainte Chapelle, and under the vaulted roof of the old abbey of Saint Denis there rang out the cry of the King of Arms: "God grant long life to Henry, by the Grace of God King of France and England, our Sovereign Lord!"

A fatality seemed to hang about Vincennes, for many kings died there, and many princes. On a spring day in 1574 King Charles IX of France died in the same room that had seen the death of Henry V. This young king—he was only twenty-four when he died—had ordered the Saint Bartholomew massacre, but that was only one of his many crimes. They say he died alone, abandoned by everyone except an old Huguenot nurse, cursing to the end. Cardinal Mazarin also died there, wearing his crimson robes, smiling as he distributed diamonds to his servants as a last gesture to a world which had never quite lived up to his expectations. Here too the young and brilliant Duc d'Enghien was brought after he was kidnaped from Germany by Napoleon, and at three o'clock in the morning he was led out under the moonless sky, with a lantern tied to his coat so that his executioners would know where to shoot. Ordered to kneel, he refused, saying that a Bourbon knelt only to God, and a moment later he was shot by a firing squad of sixteen men standing only a few paces away. They buried him so quickly that they had no time to look through his pockets. Twelve years after his death, when Napoleon was in exile, they dug up the body and found two hundred ducats and a gold watch. At Vincennes, too, died the spies captured by the French in the First World War. Mata Hari was shot there. She was still very beautiful, and the officer in charge of the execution squad had no heart to tell her she would be shot. Accordingly he invented a stratagem. He told her they would only pretend to shoot her, and at the moment when he raised his white handkerchief she was to drop down to the ground, pretending to be dead, and the bullets would fly harmlessly over her. Afterward she would be taken in secret to a hospital, where she would stay until the end of the war. She went smiling to the execution ground, and she was waving to the young officer when he gave the order to fire, and she seemed to be still smiling when he bent over her and gave her the *coup de grâce*. I know the story is true, for the young officer was one of my French cousins.

So they died, the kings and the princes and the spies, so that there is hardly an inch of earth at Vincennes which has not been drenched in blood. Vincennes was the headquarters of the French high command at the beginning of the Second World War: here General Gamelin prepared those battle plans which were to prove fatally ineffective, and here a few months later the Germans took command, and held parades, and sent out their execution squads, and kept their vast supplies of ammunition. It is still a military fortress, and no doubt it will remain a fortress until the end of time.

There are times, wandering through Vincennes, when I have the feeling that all French history has passed through this great fortress with its magnificent and somber tower. Power streams from the fortress walls. As the Sainte Chapelle represents all that is most delicate and shining in the French imagination, so the keep at Vincennes represents all the naked strength and fury of the French imagination at its most formidable and relentless. They are the bright and dark sides of the same coin.

PARIS

He was an old man and he had spent all his life in the service of the Church or of the king of England. He had been the English ambassador to France, Hainaut and Germany, and he knew the roads of Europe as well as any man. Dust-stained and weary, he had traveled from one inn to another in all the seasons of the year, so accustomed to being in the saddle that, as he once wrote, he felt uneasy in a chair. He was the tutor of Edward III, when the king was Prince Edward of Windsor. As Commissioner of Scottish Affairs he was sent on a dangerous mission to arrange a truce with the Scottish king. He became Dean of Wells, Bishop of Durham and High Chancellor of England. He was a man of all seasons, of great charm and accomplishment, among the wisest of men in his generation. His name was Richard Aungerville, but we know him best as Richard de Bury, the author of a book called *Philobiblon* which recounts at great length his love affair with books. He was also the first of the schoolmen to recount his love affair with Paris.

He was a tall man with a thin face and high cheekbones, and a wispy beard, not, one would have thought, a man given over to emotions. He presents himself as a man of studied calm and aristocratic tastes, accustomed to assuming burdensome responsibilities, but when he talks about Paris we can almost see the light shining in his eyes and the blood rushing to his cheeks. Writing about Paris, he can hardly contain his excitement. *"O Beate Deus Deorum in Syon—"* he begins, and it is like a trumpet blast of joy.

"O blessed God of Gods in Zion," he wrote. "What a mighty stream of pleasure made our hearts glad whenever we had leisure to visit Paris and to linger in the Paradise of the world! Our days there were always too few for the great love we bore the place! Here are the most charming libraries, more aromatic than chests of spices. Here are green orchards heavy with every kind of book, and academic meadows shaken by the tramp of scholars, benches like those of Athens, and peripatetic walks, and peaks of Parnassus, and porches of the Stoics! Here you may see Aristotle, surveyor of all arts and sciences, to whom belongs all that is most excellent in doctrine, so far as it relates to this transitory and sublunary world. There Paul reveals the mysteries, and Dionysius, who is his neighbor, arranges and distinguishes the celestial hierarchies, and the virgin Carmentis reproduces in Latin letters all that Cadmus collected in the Phoenician tongue. Indeed we did open out our purse strings, joyfully scattering our treasure and buying 'with earth and sand' books which are utterly without price."

So wrote Richard de Bury, and there is no doubting the passion behind the words. High honors had been showered on him, but they gave him no happiness—only Paris makes him shout with triumphant joy. He had traveled through Scotland, Germany, Flanders and France on the king's business, always with an escort of armed men, and with banners flying, but this too had given him no happiness. His happiness had come during the days when he slipped away from the court and wandered through the narrow streets of the Left Bank. He bought books prodigally, using the king's money as well as his own, and at enormous expense he packed and crated them and sent them to England. For him Paris was the new Jerusalem, the new Athens, and the new Rome.

When Richard de Bury first visited Paris about the year 1310, he may have encountered Dante, lean and hawk-faced, in the straw-covered Rue de Fouarre, where Pantagruel "held dispute against all the regents, professors of art and orators and did so gallantly that he overthrew them all and set them all upon their tails." He must have talked with many men who had talked with Saint Louis. In those days Nôtre Dame was white as snow, and all the great cathedrals built in the thirteenth century gleamed in the sun. It was a time when merchants were coming into prominence, and women were beginning to wear costly silks, and a new standard of beauty was appearing, more delicate and winsome than in the thirteenth century, when a certain heaviness was demanded of them. Richard de Bury mentions none of the people he met except "the virgin Carmentis," the bluestocking busy translating ancient Greek into church Latin, who seems to have been his secretary. He may have called her Carmentis to tease her, but most people would have called her Charmaine, a charming and common name of the period.

If we accompanied Richard de Bury round Paris, what would we see? Would it be unrecognizable, so vastly different from the Paris we know that we would lose our way? Probably we would find our way easily, for the old landmarks have remained unchanged. We would set our sights by the powerful towers of Nôtre Dame and the blazing gold cross crowning the spire of the Sainte Chapelle. On the Left Bank we would find huddled streets, markets everywhere, poor scholars everywhere; we would hear people talking in twenty tongues, for the students came from all over Europe and merchants and shopkeepers from their own countries had followed them. The students sat on the straw-covered floors of the colleges, while the professors sat in chairs. There were tennis courts set aside for the students, and communal kitchens. We would find bookshops in every corner, and on the stone bridge joining the Boulevard Saint Michel to the Ile de la Cité, we would find crowds of students arguing, for the bridge was a famous debating place.

As for the royal palace, it was set squarely on the island, a huge high pinnacled building shaped like a fortress, and overlooking the two small islands called "of Bussy" and "of the Jews," which have long since been attached to the Ile de la Cité. The palace at one end of the island, Nôtre Dame at the other, and in between there were huddles of houses—the houses crowding right up to the steep stairway which led to Nôtre Dame—and sometimes, for no apparent reason, the houses would fall away and give place to open fields; and so it was all over

Paris. There were plowed fields below the palace walls, gardens everywhere. The Crusaders returning from the East had brought a love for raw color, and fourteenth-century Paris was brighter than it is today. Banners flew outside the shops and from the church towers, and the greatest banners of all flew from the palace windows. On feast days, with the church bells ringing and the banners flying and the people marching in procession through the streets, Paris was a riot of color, and the colors were all the brighter because much of the city was new.

It was new because there had been a disastrous flood in the year 1296. It was the worst that Paris had ever suffered, being regarded as a visitation from God. "Men went in boats over the wall of the King's garden," wrote the chronicler. The entire Ile de la Cité was submerged, the stone bridge was swept away, and the flood waters reached up the Boulevard Saint Michel, sweeping away the tumble-down houses where the students lived. The upper stories of houses rose out of a lake a mile wide. Then the floods subsided, and the king of France, Philippe le Bel, ordered a vast reconstruction program. He took advantage of the flood by ordering that his palace should be made twice as large, and as though to offset the power of Nôtre Dame and the Sainte Chapelle on the other side of the island, he built the law courts in the neighborhood of the Sainte Chapelle, where they remain to this day.

The year 1310 was a good year to visit Paris because the reign of law was being extended, and the people were coming into their own. Only three years previously the Order of Templars had been suppressed. This powerful order had come into existence to protect the pilgrims in the Holy Land, and in the course of nearly two centuries it had gathered so much wealth into its hands that it had become a state within a state, ruling from its great fortress on the right bank of the Seine. The vaults of the fortress contained a king's ransom of treasure, and it was rumored that the Templars had obtained the gold by fraud and practiced black magic. The people of Paris went in fear of them, and certainly these knights, in their spotless white robes with a red cross embroidered on the shoulder, regarded the people with aristocratic disdain. On October 13, 1307, all the knights living in their great fortress were arrested in their beds by armed guards who had penetrated the inner gates by a trick. The king was determined to put an end to their power, and he had them thrown into prison, tortured and put to death. The people in Paris sang in the streets on the day the knights were arrested, and they sang again seven years later when they were put to death.

The king was richer by the twelve mule carts full of gold and silver found in the fortress, and Paris was richer than it had ever been. Quite suddenly, the women's dresses became gayer, and men took to wearing longer feathers in their caps, and more and more tradesmen came flocking to the city from abroad, bringing with them, among other treasures, the books which Richard de Bury purchased so avidly. Printing was far away in the future. The books he bought were all manuscripts copied by clerks, and since the demand was greater than the supply, and the clerks were well organized and demanded the highest fees, they cost him a fortune.

Paris was a city in its flowering springtide, raw and bright and feverish with new ideas, continually thrusting beyond its borders. It had the charm which is possessed only by cities which perpetually renew themselves, and which are small enough for a man to comprehend. Richard de Bury could have crossed the entire city in a leisurely afternoon, rejoicing in its vivid colors, the gay uniforms of the boatmen, the brilliantly painted shop signs, the gilded steeples. Victor Hugo, describing the Paris of this time, painted it in somber colors. For him it was a city seen under the aspect of night, at the mercy of its fears: the little winding streets, the houses leaning on one another, women screaming in the night and the black waters breaking through the crusts of ice. He shows you Paris as he saw it moonlit in the snow from the towers of Nôtre Dame, and it looks very small and pathetic like a rubbish heap. The dogs howl, the beggars weep, the blood runs in the gutters. But in fact Paris was not like this at all. Even in those days it was the gayest city in the world.

What a mighty stream of pleasure made our hearts glad whenever we had leisure to visit Paris and linger there, the Paradise of the world!

SAINT GERMAIN-DES-PRES

There are not many pleasures greater than sitting at the Café des Deux Magots and watching the world go by, especially on a spring day when the chestnut trees are in flower. The pleasure is compounded of many elements—girls passing, a great expanse of sky, the biscuit-colored wall and slate-blue tower of the church of Saint Germain-des-Prés, now shorn of its ancient magnificence but still remarkably beautiful, and never so beautiful as when the sun at midday turns the walls to a rich yellow. The traffic roars along the Boulevard Saint Germain, but on this corner of Paris there is always the illusory sense of being in a calm and secluded garden which looks out upon a Romanesque church of perfect proportions. The traffic roars, but remains unheard. There are only the church, the sky, the passing girls.

A man sitting at his marble-topped table on the sidewalk can easily fall into a trance, watching the world dance round him. We are told that if we are perfectly relaxed, and if all sounds are hushed, and if a succession of bright colors passes at regular intervals before our eyes, then the indispensable requirements for entering a trance state are achieved. So it is here. The colors are provided by the girls' dresses and faces, and the relaxation comes from the *petite tasse*, and the silence is created in the imagination. In this trance state the world is splendid, divinely fashioned, at peace with itself, at once desirable and beyond desire, for in this state of nirvana desire vanishes, giving place to something which has no name, though it is intimately associated with desire.

For hour upon hour, while the saucers mount on the table, one can spend one's time doing nothing fruitfully. There is the sensation of being in the unmoving center of the wheel. The girls pass, the skirts ripple in the wind, the faces take on that look of intense eagerness for experience which seems to be characteristic of the Latin Quarter, and their eyes grow even larger and more luminous. Withdrawn from the world, we find ourselves watching everything that passes with Buddhist calm and Christian sympathy. The shadows grow longer, night falls and we remain in a trance, for the bright lights continue to pass at regular intervals. Nirvana becomes paradise at the Deux Magots.

I do not know why this corner of Paris should be so blessed. I know no other place in Paris where there is so much excitement in the air, such a fierce flow of people. The cafés on the Boulevard Montparnasse—La Dôme, La Coupole, La Rotonde—have not this gaiety, and I doubt whether anyone has ever fallen into a trance while gazing out upon the sidewalks of the Boulevard Montparnasse. No; the true center of Paris, the silent hub of the wheel, is at the corner of the Boulevard Saint Germain and the Rue Bonaparte.

I remember coming here shortly after the war and listening to the philosopher Jean-Paul Sartre sitting at his table and proving to a small band of disciples that all things were meaningless except perhaps death, while the world wheeling around him seemed to be proving the opposite. He lived above the café and he would come down in the morning looking grumpy and surly to deliver his midnight reflections with paralyzing brilliance. No one ever dared to interrupt the flow of his discourse. He spoke French as great scholars wrote it in the seventeenth century, with every word in place and every comma and semi-colon clearly indicated, but these discourses were always hymns in praise of *le néant*—the nothingness of the soul. I used to pretend that *le néant* was the name of a fat green frog squatting on a lotus leaf, croaking like mad because he thought the leaf would sink under his weight and he would drown. Sartre never smiled. His arguments, which were always the same argument, were possessed of formidable logic and were utterly persuasive; it was quite clear that the universe was ruled by *le néant*, and it only remained to explore the interminable complexities of its rule. He held up *le néant* to the light, examined it minutely, turned it over, examined the other side, proved conclusively that neither side had any advantage over the other, and went on to turn both sides upside down. Every smiling girl seemed to prove that he was talking nonsense.

In those days Jean-Paul Sartre was something to marvel at. That severe intelligence was harnessed to a well-oiled and terrifying engine of destruction. He wrestled with his angel in such impeccable prose that one felt he was taking an unfair advantage over the whole angelic kingdom. There were momentous pauses. You would hear the whir of machinery deep down in his brain, and the gears locking together, and the sound of the engine picking up speed. Many years later I learned that he was an Alsatian, belonging to that cultural no man's land between Germany and France, which perhaps explained his worship of *le néant*. Still later, I learned that Jean-Paul Sartre was distantly related to Albert Schweitzer, who was also an Alsatian, and at that point all explanations seemed to fail.

Weary of listening to Sartre, I would leave the Deux Magots and go across the road to the Royale, where the American poet C. F. MacIntyre could usually be found. He looked like a Highland chieftain, craggy, jut-jawed, broken-nosed, droop-lidded, with a fine sweeping forehead and black hair which was usually ragged and resembled eagles' feathers glued haphazardly to his skull. I never knew anyone who could curse so outrageously or so pleasantly, and he was always cursing something. He, too, had his flock of attentive students, though they were considerably less reverent than Sartre's, being for the most part American students on the G. I. Bill, and not accustomed to reverence. They loved the man, and they loved him most when he was roaring poetry at the top of his lungs or commenting on the physical perfections or imperfections of the girls who passed his table or raging against the academic life, which had long ago lost its magic for him, though it seemed to haunt him. He told stories magnificently, and with the proper embroidery, which was constantly being renewed; and being the hopeful romantic, with no more logic than a mountain of quicksilver, he celebrated only the romantic poets, beginning with Walther von der Vogelweide and ending perhaps with Stéphane Mallarmé, whose most abstruse poems he was then translating. He had a blood-red sports car which he drove at an average speed of a hundred miles an hour.

For me MacIntyre was one of the greater sights of Paris. He stood taller than the Eiffel Tower. He roared louder than the black bulls he had loved and studied in his youth. He had a trencherman's appetite, and he knew all the obscure restaurants. He thought nothing of slapping the backside of a waitress he knew, but no one else could

slap so kindly. He had a roving eye, and the perpetual look of a dis-
enchanted romantic poet; but he wore his disenchantment as a dis-
guise. He was enchanted by everything he saw—wine, apples, food,
girls, blood-red sports cars, the work of some young poet, every face
he saw in the streets. I once went with him to the Cirque Médrano,
and he was much funnier than the clowns.

MacIntyre's philosophy was at the opposite pole to Sartre's, for
while Sartre rejoiced in his cold and immaculate intellectualism,
MacIntyre threw intellectualism overboard. For him the ultimate
truth lay in the poet's vision. The rhythms and images of poetry
were "the guts of the thing." If you peeled away all the skins of the
universe, you would find in the end, not *le néant*, but resounding
and joyful verses. And when, surprisingly, he settled down into do-
mesticity, the joy remained. He swore as hard as before, commented
as scurrilously as ever on every woman who passed his café table,
and roared with the same devilish laughter. The only difference was
that he told stories even better and rejoiced even more in the miracle
of being alive, and in Paris, now that he had a wife to share his joy.

MacIntyre is an American to the core, and more French than the
French. It is not, of course, an unusual phenomenon. Foreigners who
settle in France cannot avoid becoming French: it is something they
absorb from the light and air, the food, the customs, the shape of the
land. France makes all men Frenchmen. The Russians lose their Slav
ferocity and become as gentle as any French dove. Picasso is no longer
Catalan, and Brancusi very early in his life lost his typical Rumanian
qualities. Who any longer thinks of Modigliani as an Italian artist?

I think the most completely French person I ever knew was Constantin Brancusi. The man and the art were inseparable, and both
were French. His birds in flight have a peculiarly French clarity and
grace, a plenitude which springs directly out of a French imagination.
They are sunlit, sun-shot, rising into the air like notes of music, abstractions of abstractions, powerful and elegant. He liked to say they
were Tibetan birds, but that was his little joke. Those birds could
have come to birth nowhere else but in France.

He did not look like a sculptor. He looked like a wise old peasant,
his red face burned by the sun and made calm by age. He had a

shaggy white beard and his mustaches were yellowed by nicotine: he had thick lips and bright, darting eyes. When I knew him, he was already old, but he was powerfully muscled and could still move like lightning. But it was not his strength one remembered so much as his pervading gentleness, the sweetness of his smile.

I would pull on the bell outside the great square studio in the dead-end street and wait for a while, for he was deaf and did not always hear, and sometimes it would be five minutes before he came to the door wearing a skullcap and a loose white dressing gown, with a burnt-out cigarette at the corner of his lips. He would say he heard the last dying echoes of the bell more loudly than the first wild clattering, and it was easy to believe him. He smiled like a child.

The door led straight into the studio, a vast, white, shimmering place filled with his sculptures, the sky columns, the silver birds, the gray-blue fish, the white swans. Light, pouring through the glass roof, seemed to bathe them all in a soft opalescence, and as he flapped around in his sandals he sometimes gave the impression of a man super-intending the day of creation, for all these animals and birds were young, with the dew still on them. For a while we would sit by the iron stove, which seemed so incongruous in that setting, and then, motioning me to keep still, he would dart away to perform the first of a series of conjuring tricks. He would hurry away to a switch and set first one, then another, of his sculptures in motion, his face wrinkling with amusement as the turntables began to revolve and the room was filled with the hum of electricity. The effect was prodigious. Quite suddenly the room, which was very quiet, was flooded with fountains of life, and you could hear the beating of the wings.

There was *Leda*, a silvery white swan, slowly revolving on her white lake, swimming toward you and then moving away, vanishing and appearing again, the light scattering, splintering, clashing, so that sometimes she gave the effect of outspread wings and at other times she seemed to have buried her beak in her feathers and at still other times she was simply gliding along, lost in her meditations.

There, too, standing against the wall, were the towering birds for which he is most famous, in blue stone, silver or polished brass, usu-ally with a screen behind them to set off their glowing color. These, like the sky columns, were not intended to revolve, for they belonged to the space they enclosed and all the space above them. These swiftly rising birds and soaring columns were songs to fill all space, and so that there should be no doubt about the matter Brancusi once labeled a small silver bird—*Oiseau, projet devant être agrandi pour remplir la voûte du ciel*—and this bird, "project to be magnified until it fills the heavens," could have been carried easily in a handbag. Yet there was not the least intention to deceive: these birds were so formed that it was perfectly possible to imagine them leaping into the air and becoming emperors of space, even of the whole of space.

There was magic in that studio. Under dust covers, to protect them from oxidation, were superb shapes which resembled eggs, but were not eggs, shapes conjured out of stone and metal to suggest the stirring of life, its imperceptible beginnings. For Brancusi the bird in the egg and the bird in the fullness of flight were not strangers to each other. Once I saw him hold up an egg to the light, and there was a look of delighted amazement on his face as though he had never looked at an egg before. "One can be spellbound in adoration before the shape of an egg," he said. "Hold an egg in your cupped hands, and you can feel the life stirring in it." On another occasion I asked him whether any of his drawings had survived. He shrugged his shoulders. "Why draw?" he said. "There are too many lines. How many lines are there on the surface of an egg?" He went on a little later: "In the Middle Ages there was only one line. When a man set about decorating a missal, the line was known from the beginning and he simply drew his pencil round the thing he saw, but we—we see nothing and so we invent everything with our lines. In the Middle Ages religion dictated the lines, but we have no religion any more, and so we have to go back to beginnings."

I would follow him round the studio as he discussed his sculptures, talking about them as though they had been carved by someone else, praising some, dismissing others, pointing out their flaws. He would snatch at the dust covers, revealing an egg, a portrait, a tortoise made of wood, and once, hidden away in a corner, we came upon drawings made long ago, which he dismissed contemptuously.

In those days I used to compare him with Chinese scholars I had known, for he possessed a peculiarly Chinese sweetness and gravity, and the white dressing gown and white beard somehow lent themselves to the illusion. I know better now. Though he was born in Rumania and was nearly thirty before he came to Paris, he had spent so much of his life in France that his vision had become wholly French. He had the French love for light and pure form and the soaring line, and he would have been happiest in the Middle Ages before the High Renaissance came to destroy man's faith in God, giving him instead a precarious faith in himself. He hated the Renaissance, and raged against Michelangelo and Leonardo, for had they not destroyed the pure forms and desecrated the Holy of Holies? With their subtleties they had clouded over the simple human issues. He would shake his head like an old peasant at all the horrors committed by the court painters.

"There was a tradition of great beauty and value, but the Renaissance painters destroyed it. There was Giotto, for whom one can have only reverence, and then came the tyrant Michelangelo, who drew without religion and without feeling for the reverence of life. I have seen the Sistine Chapel. It is like a butcher's shop."

He would say these things with no desire to shock: he knew his history of art. He believed that something went wildly wrong in the Renaissance, and he could give an informed guess about what it was. Virtuosity destroyed the artists. "Their cleverness choked them to death. They could do anything and everything, and they were so pleased with themselves that they forgot the living forms, and they forgot to pray. Can you imagine Leonardo on his knees? Or Michelangelo?"

I asked him once whether he had ever traveled to the East.

"Of course I have," he answered. "I travel to the East in my imagination every night, but in the morning I make sure to come back to Paris. Yes, I made one visit to India. I went for a fortnight to build something for a maharajah's palace. I spent two days in Egypt. I saw the pyramids and the Cairo museum, and that was enough—enough to dream about for the rest of one's life. It does not matter where you go. Just because one is alive, it should be possible to produce great art anywhere in the world. Watch a bird. Watch anything that lives or breathes. Learn from the egg and from the bird's wing. Be like a child, and be sure that once you are no longer a child you are dead!"

At another time he said: "Create like a God. Command like a king. Work like a slave."

As he spoke, he would roll his home-made cigarettes, one eye cocked at his sculptures. He had a half-amused way of looking at them, as though he hoped to take them by surprise. And sometimes when he left the main studio to enter the annex where he kept some of his most precious possessions, he would give a little wave of his hand, as though he expected them to be good during his absence.

The annex was just as cluttered as the main studio, but, being narrower and smaller and full of silver birds, it gave an impression of greater urgency. Here were the uncompleted works, standing guard over the long since completed ones. Almost lost amid the clutter, on a low pedestal, so that you could gaze down upon it and brood over it, was the *Sleeping Muse*, a head without any body, with faint blue shadows for eyes and small delicate lips, pillowed there like an egg in a nest. You knew that, when you put your hand on the sleeping face, she would be warm and stirring with life.

The *Sleeping Muse* slept her long sleep, but everything around her was bursting with life. Cocks were crowing, immense silver birds were about to sail through the roof, sea animals were moving in and out of invisible waters, and this air of unrest always seemed faintly improper in the presence of the *Sleeping Muse*. Brancusi, on the contrary, was delighted with it, and he was always more at his ease in this small room than in the large studio, which acquired monumental dimensions from the sky pillars, those white columns carved to represent an endless chain of doves ascending to the sky.

So it was in this room that he would sometimes speak his more intimate thoughts or delve deeper into his early memories of Bucharest, where he worked as an apprentice cabinetmaker before he entered the local Ecole des Beaux Arts on a scholarship. He spoke often of the Rumanian lakes, but rarely of the people. Most of all he liked to talk about his early days as a sculptor.

"Those were good days, but they were also the very worst. I was a good student, and they will still show you the anatomical design I made—a muscular figure where everything was accurate down to the last vein and the last muscle. I made many portraits, and there came a day when I realized I could make a portrait in clay in twenty-four hours—not a passable portrait, but a really superb portrait, and then I knew that I was being devoured by my own facility. So I stopped making portraits, and I began to look for something immensely difficult. Then I learned that the most difficult thing of all was to reproduce—an egg.

"So I studied the egg, and everything I learned came from that study."

He talked like a peasant, but also like a man who was well aware of his fame. He understood himself. He had progressed along a singularly accurate line, not changing direction, like Picasso, at every breath of new fancy, but moving as birds fly, directly, without equivocation. The studio was full of birds flying across snowy skies; and the *Sleeping Muse* was always awakening from her sleep and falling into a trance again—the trance from which the world began.

I would leave him at dusk and wander back to Saint Germain-des-Prés like a man dazed. I saw him last in 1949. When he died, they published pictures of his studio, which had not changed in the interval, for he made few sculptures during the last years of his life. Only one thing had changed. He had found a small globe of the earth, and was often observed intently studying it. It was perhaps a new kind of egg, colored and more beautiful than all the others.

As a good Frenchman, he left all his works of art to the French people.

THE LADY OF THE UNICORN

"If there was one single thing in Paris which you would put under your arm and take away with you," she said, "what would you take?"

"Do you mean paintings?"

"Anything—anything you could put under your arm."

"You mean—I could have the *Mona Lisa*?"

"Yes, if you wanted the *Mona Lisa*."

But of course I didn't want the *Mona Lisa*. What on earth could one do with that faded and impeccable painting? I thought of some paintings of Van Gogh, and a ravishing Renoir, and the Avignon *Pietá*, and a head of Buddha in the Musée Guimet, but they looked better in their setting. I thought of the heavy, reddish-gold, jewel-encrusted crowns from Spain which were the delight of my childhood visits to the Cluny Museum, crowns suggesting barbaric power, which could be worn only by men ten feet high with beards like Leonardo da Vinci. Then I remembered that the crowns were no longer in Paris—the Germans in 1941 gave them to Franco.

"You mean—I can have anything I like?

"Then I think I'll take *The Lady of the Unicorn*, and thank you very much."

It was an obvious choice, but I cannot think of a better one. It might be difficult to carry the six panels away, but surely one of them could be carried under a stout arm. Those six tapestries hang in a circular room of their own in the Cluny Museum. They are un-believably rich and sensuous in their evocation of an eternal spring-time of the soul. Within a rain of flowers the tawny lions and snow-white unicorns guard the approaches to a celestial city, which remains invisible, though we know it is somewhere near because a young woman of dazzling beauty has just this moment stepped through its gates and presented herself to us. Attended by a maidservant and a monkey she goes through the motions of enjoying for our delectation each of her five senses. In a final panel we see her emerging from a tent of blue damask painted with little golden flames, and we see her opening a jewel box representing the consummation of all the senses. Over the blue tent there are the words: *A mon Seul Désir*.

No more charming wedding gift has ever been conceived, but who gave the gift? No one knows for sure, though it is thought that the tapestries were woven about the year 1509 at the order of Jean de Chabannes-Vandenesse for his betrothed, Claude De Viste. Scholars have shown that the Viste armorial bearings appear on the banners in the tapestry. Beyond this, there are only mysteries. We do not know the name of the artist who drew the cartoons, or where the tapestry was woven, or who bought it. It has been in the possession of the

Cluny Museum for a hundred years, but during that time very little has been learned about it, and a comparable tapestry has never been found. Suddenly and inexplicably we are confronted with perfection.

When the tapestry was being woven, Botticelli, Raphael and Leonardo were alive and in the full tide of their genius; Nithart was painting the Isenheim Altar; the Fontainebleau painters and Jean Clouet in France were producing major works, and the style of the High Renaissance was reaching toward its peak. The sensuous beauty of the world was being celebrated as never before, and the unrelenting imagination was given full play to describe the world in its most brilliant manifestations of beauty and clarity. The world existed for men's enjoyment: its fruits and flowers were to be examined, minutely and lovingly depicted, never plucked until they had been caressed with the eyes and submitted to the patient exploration of the senses. Man was the measure of all things, but though the world was secular, the rituals of life, as in the medieval romances, possessed a sacerdotal quality, for all things were holy by virtue of their beauty. Therefore the senses, by enabling us to perceive the world, possessed a quality of holiness.

There was, of course, nothing new in this attitude toward the senses. Duns Scotus, and many other medieval churchmen, had spoken of the senses as the vehicles by which men approach to God. What was new in the High Renaissance was the conception of human love, divinely inspired, obeying its own visible rituals and sustained by its own precarious powers, and by its very existence dispersing the dark and mysterious clouds. Love, flowing through the senses, illuminated the world.

So it is that the six tapestries of *la Dame à la licorne* have a very special importance. They stand at the heart of the mystery. They describe a particular vision, a delighted awareness of the infinite complexity of things, a sense of the permanent glory of the earth. All is freshness and peace. Against a ruby-colored dawn—it is the same color as the background of the Blue Virgin at Chartres—this unknown virgin of the tapestries quietly exults in the enjoyment of her senses. In one tapestry she plays the organ; in another she smells a flower; in others she holds up a mirror, feeds a hawk, and touches the white horn of a unicorn; and all these actions are performed according to a slow ritual of the dance of the senses. Her purposes are serious, her features grave, and she is wholly absorbed in her contemplations, which are represented by the soaring birds, the flowers and leaves hovering in her sky, and the animals serenely wandering through the forests of creation. Rabbits, panthers, monkeys, goats and sheep walk across those ruby-colored heavens completely fearless of one another. Her imagination is displayed in an intense awareness of the living forms which fill every inch of the tapestry. Not until we come to the great court carpets made to the order of the Persian Emperor Shah Abbas seventy years later shall we see such an opulent display of flowers seen as forces moving through creation.

One of the tapestries, called "The Sense of Taste," is so far superior to the others that it stands apart. Here the beauty of the design and the opulence of the colors are almost too dazzling. Wearing a gown of dull gold, the virgin stands in the center of her enchanted island with a hawk perched on her gloved left hand, while from a golden chalice held by a kneeling maidservant robed in blue she delicately picks some golden grain to offer the hawk, which has just at that very moment settled on her finger. The golden grain will lie on the hawk's tongue, and all the other birds and animals of her imagination will come to feed on the grain, which will never touch her lips. It is magic grain, and its taste is magical. So for once the unknown artist departs from the scheme of representing the five senses by invoking the taste of creation.

The Lady of the Unicorn is really a portrait of Paradise, the same Paradise which is described by the poet Charles Peguy when he wrote in *The Good Gardeners:*

Well, said God, I admire my French gardeners—they know how to plant well,
They seek out the living waters, they go to the secret springs.
They know how to make bread and wine, and how to enjoy them,
And they are especially good at cultivating the gardens of the soul.
They have brought me flowers and fruit in secret, and I approve of them.
They are the true inventors of gardens: I shall make them the gardeners of the King.
I order my Frenchmen to design the gardens of Paradise.

INDEX

INDEX

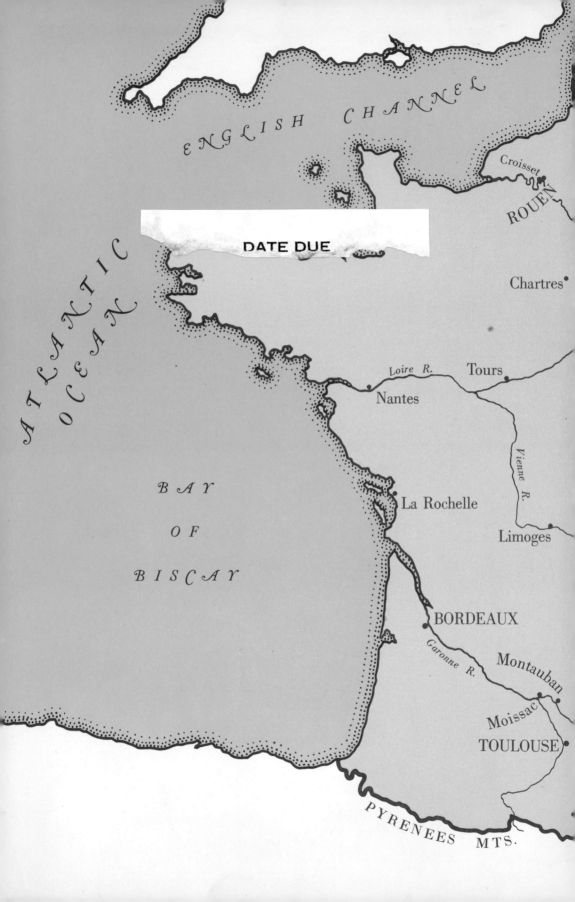